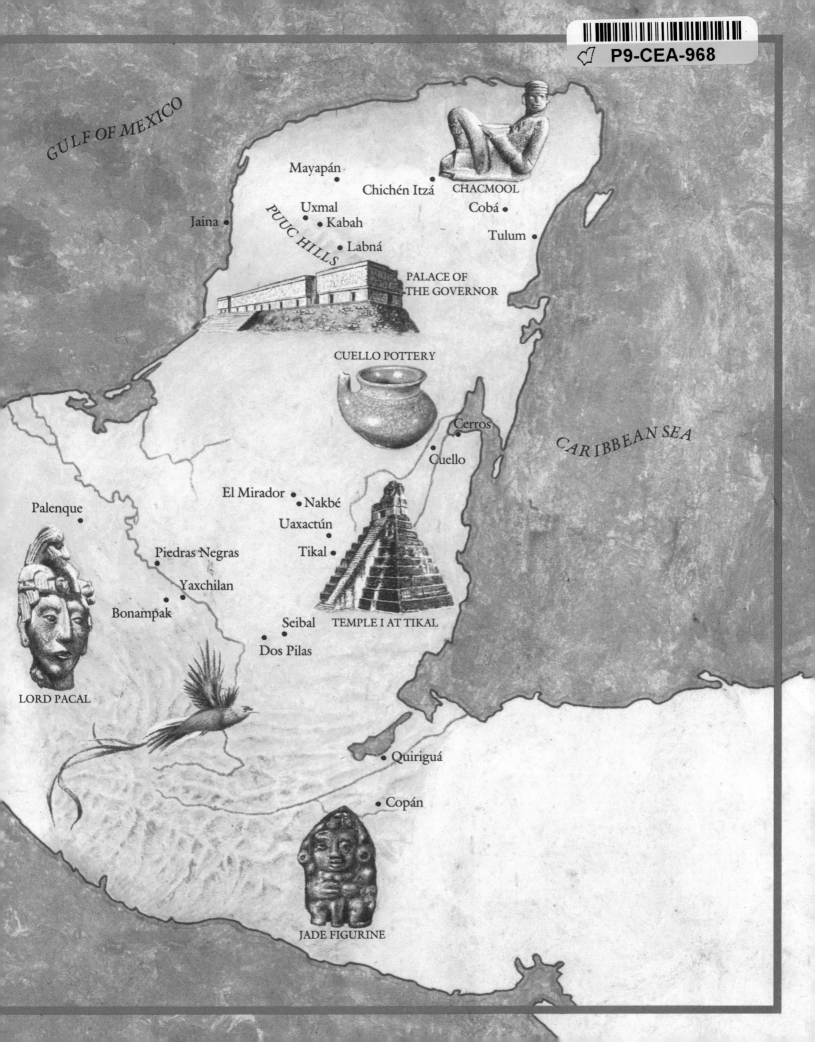

GULF OF MEXICO

Mayapán

Chichén Itzá

CHACMOOL

Uxmal

Cobá

Jaina

PUUC HILLS

Kabah

Tulum

Labná

PALACE OF
THE GOVERNOR

CUELLO POTTERY

Cerros

CARIBBEAN SEA

Cuello

El Mirador

Nakbé

Palenque

Uaxactún

Piedras Negras

Tikal

Yaxchilan

Bonampak

TEMPLE I AT TIKAL

Seibal

Dos Pilas

LORD PACAL

Quiriguá

Copán

JADE FIGURINE

Cover: A stunning example of Maya artistry, this painted ceramic figurine—found with thousands of others in graves on the island of Jaina off the northwest Yucatan coast—captures the grim visage of a Maya noble; his accouterments include an elaborate headdress and a beaded necklace. The background photograph shows Chichén Itzá's great temple-pyramid, dubbed El Castillo, "the castle," by its Spanish discoverers.

End paper: Painted on bark paper by the artist Paul Breeden, the map delineates the lands of Central America ruled by the ancient Maya, stretching from the Yucatan Peninsula in the north to the Sierra Madre along the Pacific coast. Breeden also painted the vignettes illustrating the timeline on pages 160-161.

THE
MAGNIFICENT
MAYA

Library of Congress Cataloging in Publication Data
The Magnificent Maya / by the editors of Time-Life Books.
      p. cm.—(Lost civilizations)
   Includes bibliographical references and index.
   ISBN 0-8094-9879-0 (trade)
   ISBN 0-8094-9880-4 (lib. bdg.)
   1. Mayas—Antiquities.
   2. Central America—Antiquities.
   3. Mexico—Antiquities.
I. Time-Life Books. II. Series.
F1435.M35   1993
972.81 016—dc20   92-39965

The Consultants:
John B. Carlson, director of the Center for Archaeoastronomy in College Park, Maryland, has conducted extensive textual and fieldwork studies of Maya art and hieroglyphic writings, with a focus on astronomy in Maya culture.

Arthur Demarest, professor of anthropology at Vanderbilt University, has served as project director for numerous excavations in Maya territory. His discoveries at Dos Pilas have provided new insights into the downfall of Classic Maya civilization.

William L. Fash, Jr., professor of anthropology at Northern Illinois University, is director of the Copán Acropolis Archaeological Project. He has written and lectured widely on Copán and appeared in a number of television documentaries about the Maya.

Norman Hammond, professor of archaeology at Boston University, has directed a multiyear excavation and study of the early Maya site of Cuello. He is a research associate in Maya archaeology for Harvard's Peabody Museum.

Jeff Karl Kowalski, professor of art history at Northern Illinois University, served as principal investigator of a 1992 excavation at Uxmal. His studies focus on art and architecture in the northern Maya area.

THE
MAGNIFICENT
MAYA

By the Editors of Time-Life Books

TIME-LIFE BOOKS, ALEXANDRIA, VIRGINIA

CONTENTS

CITIES BURIED IN FORESTS, DESOLATE, WITHOUT A NAME

Lost and forgotten, the city lay wrapped in greenery, smothered by the forest it had once commanded. Its palaces and temples were overhung by mahogany and ceiba trees, webbed with vines, walled about with ferns and shrubs. Tropical rains lashed at the crumbling surfaces of stone and stucco; roots pried apart great structures that had been raised by armies of workers. By night, jaguars prowled the urban spaces, their hoarse roars punctuating the hours of darkness. By day, the city's voices were parrot shrieks and the calls of monkeys traveling through the treetops. The carved effigies of gods stared out into the steamy jungle, where not a single human being remained to worship them.

This, in its afterlife, was the place called Copán, sited along a river in the wilds of western Honduras. For a millennium its existence had remained spectral, a memory dimmed to the point of invisibility. Europeans had come across it soon after their arrival in the New World, but had taken little note of the ruins except to mention them in a few arcane reports on the area. Then, in the year 1839, an American lawyer-diplomat named John Lloyd Stephens and an English artist, Frederick Catherwood, breached the jungle fastness and rediscovered the miracle of Maya civilization.

Stephens and Catherwood were veteran travelers and had never been put off by rough country—although this particular coun-

A huge stucco mask glowers from the side of a ruined 1,500-year-old Maya temple virtually hidden by jungle in the Petén region of Guatemala. Hundreds of other forgotten Maya sites in Mexico and Central America await excavation and study like this one.

try was more formidable than anything they had ever seen. They made their way into the dank Honduran rain forest with the help of local guides, riding their mules along rivers haunted by the crocodile-like caiman, following narrow tracks through mountains, pressing ever deeper into a green kingdom glinting with hummingbirds and festooned with orchids. Their hope, inspired by some obscure books they had read, was to reach "great cities beyond the Vale of Mexico, buried in forests, ruined, desolate, without a name," as Stephens wrote. The few existing descriptions of these cities were so vague, however, that the two adventurers were braced for disappointment. And indeed, their first glimpse of Copán—an ancient local name for the valley and nearby river—was unimpressive: a wall of cut stone, well made but frail compared with the massive fortifications they had seen during their Old World travels. "We ascended by large stone steps, in some places perfect, and in others thrown down by trees which had grown up between the crevices, and reached a terrace, the form of which it was impossible to make out, from the density of the forest in which it was enveloped."

As a guide cleared a path with his machete, they came to a structure that resembled a pyramid, although the covering of vegetation masked its precise shape. Then, amid the thickets, they spotted a four-sided stone column—a freestanding monument of a type known as a stele. It measured 13 feet in height and about three feet on each side, and its surfaces were densely adorned with relief carvings. On the front was the image of a man, exotically costumed, his expression ferocious. The sides were devoted to hieroglyphs—pictorial writing inscribed with a deft-

A cloud-wreathed mountain towers over the Maya city of Palenque in this picture showing three of its huge stone pyramids topped by temples (right) and its palace (far left). This 19th-century lithograph was based on drawings made at the site by pioneering English explorer-artist Frederick Catherwood.

ness that Stephens judged equal to the script on the finest monuments of the ancient Egyptians. He had no idea what the glyphs signified or who the fierce figure was. Their guide declared the column to be an idol. Pushing on through the forest tangle, the explorers located 14 more steles, "one displaced from its pedestal by enormous roots, another locked in the close embrace of branches of trees and almost lifted out of the earth; another hurled to the ground, and bound down by huge vines and creepers." Each set of carvings offered fresh mysteries.

They eventually made their way back to the large pyramid-shaped building and laboriously climbed its steps, which were ornamented with even more strange sculptures. Struggling up, over, and then down the other side, they came upon more steps and found at the top, almost 100 feet above the jungle floor, a broad terrace. The two men sat on its edge and looked out over the sea of trees. Stephens later recollected the moment. Copán "lay before us like a shattered bark in the midst of the ocean, her masts gone, her name effaced, her crew perished, and none to tell whence she came, to whom she belonged, how long on her voyage, or what caused her destruction." The local Indians could not enlighten the travelers. When asked who had built this city, they replied, *"Quién sabe?"* (Who knows?)

But Stephens and Catherwood had lifted the veil. In two separate trips they visited more than three dozen ruined cities, some of which had been so completely enveloped by the jungle that they were unknown even to the locals. When they returned home and published their findings, their words and pictures ignited public interest in the secrets of the Middle American tropics and inspired a multitude of investigations. Soon the identity of the builders of Copán and other settlements became clear: They were the forebears of the Maya Indians still living by the millions in that land. Moreover, the impressive list of sites that Stephens and Catherwood had logged was but a fraction of what those ancient people had wrought—less than a quarter of perhaps 200 sizable cities constructed in the Maya time of glory. As many as 20 of these may have had populations exceeding 50,000. Their collective domain embraced the entire Yucatan Peninsula, parts of the modern-day Mexican states of Tabasco and Chiapas, all of Guatemala and Belize, and the western portions of Honduras and El Salvador—125,000 square miles in all.

A lithograph of another Catherwood drawing pictures local Indians resting before a magnificent 20-foot-high stone archway leading into the Palace of the Governor at Uxmal, a great center of Maya culture on the Yucatan Peninsula. Atop the arch and along its sides are carved stone masks with the elongated snout of the Maya rain god, Chac.

It was a realm of great variety. In the south were volcanic highlands cleft by deep gorges and rift valleys. To the north and east of the mountains lay heavily forested lowlands where 160 inches of rain could fall in a year, draining into the Gulf of Mexico and the Caribbean through great river systems. Farther north was the drier, flatter terrain of the Yucatan Peninsula, a vast platform of limestone covered by low trees and scrub, with little water beyond what could be brought up from scattered sinkholes, where the soft rock had caved in to create deep, circular chasms.

In its different guises, the area was one of the least hospitable places in the entire hemisphere, its physical difficulties compounded by the presence of all sorts of stinging insects and poisonous snakes, spiders, and scorpions. Nonetheless, the ancient Maya managed to thrive, swelling in number to perhaps as many as 10 or even 20 million at their peak. In the process, they shaped a civilization of

Natives of the Yucatan village of Bolonchen clamber up and down an 80-foot wooden ladder to draw water at a subterranean well in a dramatic lithograph based on one of Catherwood's drawings of Indian life at the time of his travels. During the dry season water is still drawn today from underground supplies, which seep through the porous limestone that underpins the region and pool in natural sinkholes like this one.

extraordinary vitality. First emerging as an identifiable society about 1000 BC, they entered a kind of golden age around AD 250, mastering techniques of intensive farming, spreading the tentacles of their trade networks far and wide, perfecting their distinctive architecture of steep-sided pyramids, stone ball courts, and corbel-arched palaces, and establishing elaborate political and social hierarchies.

At the same time, they expanded the reach of the human mind, making use of a range of powerful intellectual tools. Of all the ancient cultures that flourished in the Americas, the Maya were virtually alone in devising a fully developed writing system. They employed a complex arrangement of interlocking calendars *(pages 30-31)* and several other time cycles to record important historical dates, keep track of astronomical events, and gaze across immense vistas of the past and future, imagining times that seem remote to even the most farsighted of modern cosmologists. Their computations and recordkeeping were based on a supple arithmetical system that included a symbol for zero, unknown to the Greeks and Romans, and their precision in celestial observations far exceeded that of any other contemporary civilization.

All of this and more marked the Maya as a people of genius. But by about AD 900—earlier in some places, later in others—a decline had set in, most likely caused by a malign mix of factors that may have included overpopulation and a corresponding destruction of environmental resources necessary to their survival, the disruptive ambitions of rulers, and invasion by aggressive neighbors. The cities in the southern and central lowlands emptied, and the hub of Maya civilization shifted northward to Yucatan. By around 1450, the old order, with its elaborate ideology and mechanisms of statecraft, collapsed there as well.

Much of the Maya story has been gleaned from the physical remains of their world—the temples and tombs and dwellings that continue to emerge from forest hiding places. Yet so much more waits to be found that researchers must be ever prepared to revise their thinking in the light of new discoveries. In 1991, for example, archaeologists working in Belize came across a stele bearing symbols that they thought might correspond to a date of 146 BC, which would make it the oldest Maya stele ever found and the earliest evidence of any sort of historical recordkeeping in Maya territory. The markings were badly eroded, however, and other scholars have disputed the interpretation; nevertheless, other recent discoveries

AN ARTIST WITH A CURSE

The English artist Frederick Catherwood seemed to have been born under an unlucky star. Of his numerous drawings and watercolors of Old World subjects, many remain unpublished, and others have been lost. And although his fine images of Maya ruins, such as the one below in which he appears on the right in front of a temple, would bring him lasting fame, they nearly cost him his life. Published in three popular works, two in collaboration with Catherwood's travel companion, John Lloyd Stephens, the paintings give little hint of the hardship the artist endured. In the jungle he contracted malaria and suffered recurring

bouts of fever. "He was wan and gaunt," wrote Stephens, "lame, like me, from the bites of insects; his face was swollen and his left arm hung with rheumatism, as if paralyzed." At one point, Catherwood had to be carried on the shoulders of Indians. "It seemed almost as if I were following his bier," Stephens reported. But Catherwood recovered.

In a building in New York where the artist had set up a profitable panorama of Thebes and Jerusalem, the two men exhibited paintings, drawings, and artifacts brought back from Maya country. A fire broke out, destroying everything. But a crueler fate lay in store: Some years later, returning to America from England, Catherwood drowned at sea when his ship collided with another.

tend to support the notion that Maya society rose to a sophisticated level far earlier than had been imagined.

Such new information often adds to the challenge for those seeking to decipher Maya writing—the 800 or so types of hieroglyphic symbols that were carved into steles and other monuments, inscribed on wall panels and wooden lintels, and painted on pottery and in bark-paper codices or books. Until the mid-20th century, this glyphic code resisted almost every effort at decryption. Some scholars suspected that a huge wealth of knowledge about Maya life and history was locked away in the pictorial language. Others preferred to think that the glyphs did not record mundane matters but instead expressed mystical ideas about the workings of the cosmos—in particular, meditations on astrology and the flow of time, guided by what one scholar called calendar priests. This view of the Maya as time worshipers was built on a narrow foundation: For decades, the only symbols that could be deciphered dealt with numbers, time, and astronomical cycles.

But when the mystery of the writing finally began to give way, the

glyphs painted a much more elaborate picture. The Maya had chosen to memorialize not just their mythology and their knowledge of things heavenly but also the very earthly details of politics and warfare, of social position and personal glory. To modern sensibilities, the revelations have at times been shocking. These were a people for whom the deliberate shedding of one's own blood—in the most ghastly of fashions—was a sacred, world-sustaining act, and for whom the apparently cruel treatment of captured enemies was behavior imbued with a sense of higher purpose. But above all, they were a people with a keen regard for their own history and heritage, who had clearly wanted to be remembered. How their story has indeed been reclaimed is itself a fascinating tale, with its share of wasted opportunities and unexpected breakthroughs, of misguided speculations and carefully reasoned theories. And as any of today's investigators will attest, the plot continues to unfold, as more and more discoveries are made in remote jungle areas.

The Maya calculated that the present universe was formed on a date that corresponds in the Julian calendar to August 11, 3114 BC, and their system of cosmic cycles dictated that it would end on December 21, AD 2012. But in reality the death of the world as they knew it came in the 16th century, with the arrival of Spanish soldiers, friars, and colonists, all determined to remake the New World according to their beliefs and appetites.

The first contact between these two vastly different cultures was brief, involving no less a figure than Christopher Columbus. Although the great mariner never landed on the shores of Middle America, in 1502 he approached the northern coast of Honduras on his fourth voyage to what he still thought were the Indies. Near the island of Guanaja he encountered a trading canoe, eight feet wide and apparently carved from a single huge tree trunk. In the vessel were a number of men, women, and children, along with piles of goods arranged under a canopy of woven mats. The cargo included copper plates, stone hatchets, wooden swords edged with razor-sharp flints, pottery, cacao beans, and brightly patterned cloths of woven cotton. Reports differ as to whether the meeting was amicable and gifts were exchanged or the Europeans merely helped themselves to what they wanted, but in any event they soon sailed on, giving little emphasis to the incident in later accounts of the voyage. But they had learned one thing of lasting significance about these people: They came from a place they called Maia or Maiam—the source of the word *Maya*.

A later meeting proved more fateful. In 1517, three Spanish ships on a raiding expedition for slaves traveled around the northern coast of Yucatan, stopping at one island where they looted temples, and eventually ending up on the mainland. The 110 Spaniards were thereupon attacked by masses of warriors, but the soldiers managed to drive the Maya fighters off with the ships' artillery. When the Spaniards returned to their already well secured base in Cuba and displayed prizes that included ornaments made of low-grade gold, the die was cast: There were clearly riches to be won on the mainland, and no one would be allowed to stand in the way of their being claimed for the Spanish crown.

Within four years, the great Aztec empire in central Mexico had fallen to Hernán Cortés, who then dispatched one of his captains south to conquer the territory now encompassed by Guatemala and

El Salvador—a task accomplished quickly and brutally. Cortés himself marched farther east into present-day Honduras in 1524, with the Maya scattering before him, and in 1526 another conquistador began the process of subduing Yucatan. There, however, the defenders proved to be more of a challenge. A Spanish chronicler described one attack by the Maya in which they appeared with "quivers of arrows, poles with their tips hardened by fire, lances with points of sharp flints, two-handed swords of very strong woods inset with obsidian blades, whistles, and beating the shells of great turtles with deer horns." Nevertheless, in that battle as in most others, the better-armed Spaniards prevailed. The conquest of Yucatan was largely completed by 1547, although some of the Maya fled into the gloomy forests of the interior, where they and their descendants managed to hold out for another 150 years.

War and wildfire epidemics of such European diseases as measles, smallpox, and influenza—against which the local people had no natural immunity—took the lives of millions of the Maya during this period. Most of the survivors were stripped of their lands and yoked to Spanish estates as little better than slaves. The European overlords were also determined to eradicate the Indians' religion. Temples were torn down and shrines smashed. Friars punished suspected idolators by whipping them, stretching their joints with pulleys, and scalding them with boiling water. In Yucatan, the leader of these activities to "cleanse" the pagans was a Franciscan named Diego de Landa.

Landa was a complex man, a zealot who believed that success in his ecclesiastical labors required a thorough knowledge of the world he intended to reform. In the years after his arrival in 1549, he became fluent in the local language and devoted much of his time to learning about native life—customs and rituals, the Maya calendar, farming methods, food, drink, clothing, and much more. He also visited the ruined cities, already long since abandoned, and saw that Yucatan had once enjoyed a much more "prosperous time, when so many and such remarkable buildings were built." The abundant hieroglyphs in particular intrigued him, and he discovered that some Indians could still read the old script. One afternoon, he sat with an informant and pronounced various letters in the Spanish alphabet, asking the Indian to draw glyphs representing the same sounds. He assumed that Maya writing, like Spanish and other Western languages, was purely alphabetic and would lend itself to straightforward match-ups between picture-symbols and letters. In this he was wrong, and the secret of the Maya inscriptions remained intact for centuries more; but Landa had unwittingly bequeathed to posterity invaluable information that would ultimately help crack the code.

Landa also discovered that the Maya had an entire literature, some of it evidently reaching deep into their past. In a town 40 miles southeast of the Spanish-founded city of Mérida on the Yucatan coast, he came across a cache of nearly 30 hieroglyphic books. They were lovely objects, their delicate calligraphy painted in black and red ink on paper made from the inner bark of the fig or mulberry tree and covered with gesso, a plasterlike compound that formed a smooth surface; the pages were folded like a screen and covered with jaguar skin. Although these volumes could have proved a tremendous re-source for his researches, Landa's religious fervor came tragically to the fore. He somehow determined that the Maya had filled the works with esoteric lore, and since "they contained nothing in which there were not to be seen superstitions and falsehoods of the devil, we burned them all, which they took most grievously, and which gave them great pain."

His treatment of people was no less severe. During a three-month inquisition carried out under his direction in 1562, almost 5,000 Indians were tortured and 158 died. Landa was summoned back to Spain on charges of exceeding his authority. While awaiting disposition of his case, he composed a lengthy treatise on the Maya, setting down all that he had learned about their culture, including the supposed alphabet system. Perhaps he intended the document as a guide to other missionaries, but it simply disappeared, probably into church archives. As for official questions about his soul-saving tac-tics, he was exonerated and sent back to Yucatan as a bishop.

The conquest period saw the disappearance of much else

besides Landa's trove of information on the Maya. In every way possible, Indian culture was suppressed. Ancient expertise in mathematics and astronomy faded away, European-style writing became the required form of literacy, and knowledge of the age-old hieroglyphs withered. Meanwhile, vines and creepers continued to spread over the great stepped pyramids and stone palaces. Some of the greatest of the ancient cities were never even glimpsed by the Spaniards; they lay in the rain forest of the southern lowlands, a region that attracted few colonists. Indeed, some were to sleep in a cobwebbed spell cast by time, abandoned, completely isolated, not to be visited by anyone until the 1980s.

Only a century or so after the coming of the Europeans, the glories of the Maya past continued not even as a memory. Few outsiders sensed that the deserted ruins scattered from the flatlands of Yucatan to the mountain valleys farther south had sprung from a

Studies of Maya building techniques, these 18th-century drawings by Italian architect and expedition leader Antonio Bernasconi are the first to show cross sections and ground plans of Maya temples. Curiously, Bernasconi left out the distinctive roof decorations called combs present on many Maya temples.

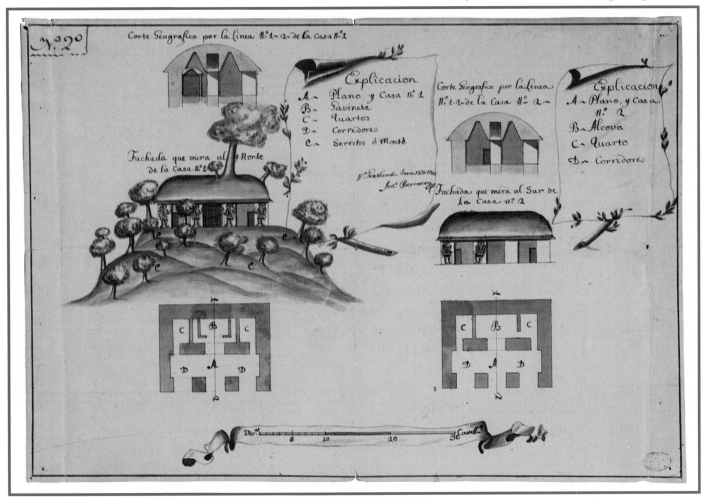

single civilization that endured for more than a millennium; nor did anyone imagine that a culture worthy of comparison with those of the ancient Egyptians and Greeks had flourished in this difficult tropical realm. But such a secret could not last. Beginning in the late 18th century and continuing to the present day, the forgotten Maya have emerged into the light again, retrieved through the efforts of a remarkable assortment of investigators—adventurers and romantics as well as professional archaeologists and scholars. As an exercise in historical inquiry, the search for the Maya has been anything but orderly, and in the early years especially, fantasy often overwhelmed the facts. But if the truth was slow in taking shape, it proved hardly less compelling than some of the wilder dreams.

One of the first searchers was Antonio del Rio, a Spanish army captain stationed in Guatemala. In 1786 he was assigned by a government official to examine some ruins near the town of Santo Domingo de Palenque, about 220 miles northwest of Guatemala City. The official had heard about this place from a priest and had made several unsatisfactory attempts to get more information. Finally he sent del Rio there, instructing him to measure and describe the buildings, estimate the age of the complex, and, if possible, learn something about its founders and the reasons for its downfall.

Del Rio had no archaeological experience, but he was a man of energy and determination. When he reached the site, on hilly ground in a rain forest, he found it so thickly overgrown with trees and underbrush that he could see no more than a few feet in front of him. He commandeered a force of about 80 Indians, who spent 16 days clearing and burning vegetation to bring the ruins into view.

Palenque, as it came to be known, covered several square miles. Many of its buildings had crumbled away to almost nothing, but some of the finest still retained their ancient grandeur. Mounted on low pyramids were four splendidly decorated temples adorned with stucco reliefs, hieroglyphs, and, in three of them, tableaux showing religious ceremonies. A palace, sectored into a maze of halls, rooms, courtyards, and other spaces, overlooked the city on an earthen platform measuring 300 by 240 feet.

The army captain diligently dug and measured, gathering a few plaques and assorted artifacts as he went. An

The earliest known drawing of the central scene on a magnificent carved panel in the Temple of the Sun at Palenque (below), *done in 1784 by the Spaniard José Calderón, differs strikingly from the detail-revealing photograph of a plaster cast of the panel at right made by the 19th-century Englishman Alfred P. Maudslay. Calderón rendered the jaguar's head on the shield as a decorative contrivance and failed to note that the fierce-looking men are standing upon the backs of two abjectly kneeling captives, whom he rendered merely as designs.*

artist he had brought along also made sketches of the most striking remains. After a few weeks of work, a report was assembled and submitted to the government. Del Rio had been unable to reach any conclusion about the city's builders, but he believed that Palenque was culturally akin to the more accessible ruins in Yucatan.

Del Rio's account was sent to Spain and, like Landa's treatise, sank into archival obscurity. A copy had been made, however, and by mysterious means reached the hands of a London bookseller, who published it in 1822. Few people read it, but the Maya world no longer lay entirely in the shadows.

Less than 20 years after del Rio's expedition, another small step toward recognition was taken by Guillermo Dupaix, a Dutchman who had spent decades in Mexico serving in the Spanish army and was now a retired captain of dragoons. Well educated and well connected, he was fascinated by antiquities and managed in 1804 to win a royal appointment from Charles IV of Spain to investigate pre-Hispanic sites in Mexico. Between 1805 and 1808, Dupaix traveled throughout Mexico with an artist in tow, visiting ruins and occasionally attempting modest excavations. The only noteworthy Maya city on his itinerary was Palenque, described to him by the very same priest who had spoken of the site to del Rio's superior. Getting there was an exhausting experience, even for a military man used to hardship. "The space which we had to traverse," Dupaix later wrote, "is scarcely passable for any other animal than a bird; the road winding through mountains and over precipices, which we crossed sometimes on the backs of mules and sometimes on foot. Our only vehicle was a litter or a hammock, and we were compelled to pass the streams which intersected our route by bridges rudely formed of trees."

But when he finally reached his goal, Dupaix's reaction verged on rapture. The architecture enthralled him, especially its ornamentation: paintings that swarmed with birds, flowers and fruit, lovely stucco plaques, dramatic bas-reliefs. Commenting on the human figures in the reliefs, he wrote: "Their attitudes display great freedom of limb, with a certain expression of dignity. Their dress, though sumptuous, never wholly covers the body; their heads are decorated with helmets, crests, and spreading plumes." All of these figures, he noted, had flattened heads, which convinced him that the Indians now living in the area could not be descendants of the people who had built and lived in Palenque. His somewhat wonderstruck conclusion was that the city must have been the creation of an entirely unknown and vanished race. Because of political turmoil in Mexico and the outbreak of the Napoleonic Wars overseas, however, Dupaix's report on pre-Hispanic ruins never reached the Spanish king. It languished in government files for some years before being published in Mexico and Europe—in so sloppy and disjointed a form, however, that it failed to stir any significant interest.

The trickle of visitors to Palenque continued, one of whom offered a particularly bizarre explanation for the

WALDECK THE GREAT

Jean Frédéric Waldeck—whose nationality has never been clearly established—was as adept at inventing a past for the Maya as he was at creating one for himself. A self-styled count (and sometime duke), he was an accomplished raconteur who became a legend during his long lifetime—110 years by some accounts. He regaled his listeners with heroic tales of desert escapes, brushes with death, and deeds of service under Napoleon in Egypt. He was married three times, taking his third wife when he was in his eighties and fathering a son by her.

A decade before Catherwood sketched the Maya ruins, Waldeck *(right)* was producing his own views of the monuments and glyphs. Just where he received his artistic training no one knows, but

Waldeck's rendering of glyphs on the Temple of Inscriptions at Palenque shows his penchant for finding Old World influences in Maya script. The elephant heads and cuneiform signs are strictly products of his imagination. The "elephant," in fact, represents the long-nosed rain god, Chac.

he had enough resolve and talent to spend a year in the jungle in the early 1830s drawing. His dramatic paintings were published in 1838. Unfortunately, Waldeck's strong conviction that the Maya had developed from Old World stock distorted his perceptions and drove him to see nonexistent Egyptian, Greek, Mesopotamian, and Hindu influences in the glyphs (below). In a pictorial reconstruction of a temple, he included four standing giants he claimed existed in pieces; but when archaeologists looked for them, not a trace could be found.

magnificence of what he had seen there and at other sites. Juan (originally John) Galindo was an Irish-born adventurer who had ended up in Guatemala in 1827, at the age of 25. Various factions were fighting for control of the country at the time, and Galindo managed to affiliate himself with the winning group. He was soon appointed governor of northern Guatemala and in 1831, while touring the region under his authority, made an exploratory trip to Palenque. Three years later, the government asked him to inspect Copán as well, whose existence had been known—at least locally— since the days of the Spanish conquest. Soon thereafter, he spelled out his theory in a report that played to the nationalistic pride of his Guatemalan sponsors.

Galindo believed that political power and cultural progress always move westward. In his considered opinion, the original starting point—the birthplace of world civilization—had been Central America. In very ancient times, a prodigiously gifted race had lived there, but some disaster had befallen them. The survivors journeyed west to Asia and points beyond, establishing a series of successor civilizations—Chinese, Hindu, Chaldean, and Egyptian. Meanwhile, culture bloomed anew at places like Copán and Palenque, but not so gloriously as before. Nor did it last long. A process that Galindo likened to aging had weakened the people of the region, which accounted for their inability to repel the invading Spaniards—who, in his judgment, compared with the original inhabitants, had been no better than barbarians.

Galindo himself soon met a tragic end. In 1840, the combined armies of Honduras and Nicaragua defeated the federal forces of Guatemala, and Galindo had to flee for his life. But as he passed through a Honduran village, Galindo was recognized and was promptly slaughtered with machetes. The Irish adventurer's writings too appeared headed for oblivion, but they happened to catch the eye of John Lloyd Stephens, a man who did not miss a great deal: He had also managed to get his hands on the equally obscure reports of del Rio, Dupaix, and a few others. His interest piqued, Stephens began to make plans, and the stage

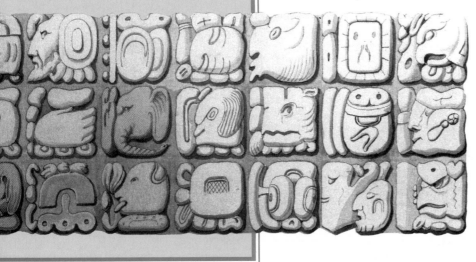

was at last set for the full-scale rediscovery of the Maya world.

Stephens always seemed destined to do great things. Born into an affluent New York family in 1805, he was a brilliant student and indefatigably curious. In his twenties he practiced law and became a force in the Jacksonian political movement, then took two years off to travel through Greece, Russia, Palestine, Egypt, and other lands, sometimes trekking into remote areas and disguising himself in native dress. When he returned to New York, he resumed his legal career but decided to try his hand at writing as well. In rapid succession, he penned four volumes on his travels. They sold so well that he gave up his original vocation.

On his way through London after his grand tour, Stephens had met Frederick Catherwood, six years his senior. Like Stephens, Catherwood had been raised in comfortable circumstances, received an excellent education, and traveled extensively in Europe and the Near East, sketching ruins and exotic locales—an amusement that soon became a passion. Af-

AGONIES OF TRAVEL IN YUCATAN

The early scholars and artists who penetrated the Yucatan Peninsula and Central America found travel to the Maya ruins excruciating. At best it meant being rocked and shaken for days in an Indian-born litter like artist Jean Frédéric Waldeck, who pictured himself in the lithograph above jouncing in such a conveyance. Worse was the commonest form of travel, riding for days on bony, balky mules. Worse still was being carried in a chair strapped to a porter's back—as is shown in the engraving at right of Frenchman Désiré Charnay—along terrifyingly narrow and treacherous mountain trails while getting soaked to the skin by tropical downpours.

Things were little better when the explorers reached the ruins. There they became victims of all the malice of tropical nature. "The rain was incessant," Charnay complained. "The damp seems to penetrate the very marrow of our bones; a vegetable mould settles on our hats which we are obliged to brush off daily; we live in mud, we are covered in mud, we breathe in mud; the ground is so slippery that we are as often on our backs as on our feet." Once Charnay awakened to find 200 "cold and flat insects the size of a large cockroach" in his hammock, 30 of which clung to his body and bit him painfully.

ter serving as the artist on an archaeological expedition to Egypt, he moved to New York. His intention was to practice architecture there, but soon he and Stephens were working on the notion of producing a travel book on the mysterious ruins of the Middle American tropics—a surefire publishing success if indeed the ruins were anything like what Stephens had read about in the few published reports.

To help defray expenses, Stephens used his political connections to gain an appointment as a diplomatic agent of the United States government, a role that involved no significant duties but would lend the two explorers leverage in any dealings with officialdom. They set out from New York in October 1839. About a month later, after a wilderness journey that Stephens would describe in wonderfully vivid prose, they reached Copán, discovered the steles, climbed the pyramid, and saw that they had come upon a kind of travel-writer's mother lode.

"It is impossible to describe the interest with which I explored these ruins," Stephens later wrote. "The ground was entirely new;

there were no guidebooks or guides; the whole was a virgin soil. We could not see 10 yards before us, and never knew what we should stumble upon next. At one time we stopped to cut away branches and vines which concealed the face of a monument, and then to dig around and bring to light a fragment, a sculptured corner of which protruded from the earth. I leaned over with breathless anxiety while the Indians worked, and an eye, an ear, a foot or a hand was disentombed; and when the machete rang against the chiselled stone, I pushed the Indians away, and cleared out the loose earth with my hands."

Stephens prided himself on being a careful observer and approached the business of interpretation with lawyerly precision. Before coming to any conclusions about Copán, he wanted to gather more evidence. Traveling temporarily to Guatemala City, he and Catherwood arranged to go to Palenque, and Stephens inquired if other ruins might be found along the way. He learned of a number of sites, some buried deep in the jungle, and the two men set off on an epic journey of discovery. Much of the time, they were traveling through regions hardly ever penetrated by outsiders,

FROM THE WILDS OF YUCATAN.

RUINS OF CHICHEN-ITZA.

GRAN DISCOVERY OF CHAACMOL STATUE.

Phot. by Dr. Aug. Le Plongeon and Lady.

"as wild as before the Spanish conquest," Stephens said. At many of the sites, they were struck by stylistic resemblances to the architecture and decoration of Copán. Finally they reached what Stephens called the "mournfully beautiful" Palenque, and were quick to notice that the hieroglyphs were the same as those they had seen at Copán. Stephens was now ready to declare that "the whole of this country was once occupied by the same race, speaking the same language, or, at least, having the same written characters."

But who were those people? One possibility was that they were the heirs of some ancient Old World civilization, such as that of China or Egypt. Stephens weighed the case for an infusion of genius from across the Atlantic or Pacific and dismissed it. These ruins, he said, "are different from the works of any other known people, of a new order, and entirely and absolutely anomalous; they stand alone." Nor did he accept Galindo's cradle-of-civilization notion, or Dupaix's contention that modern-day Indians could not be descended from the builders of these now-ruined complexes. Stephens decided that the cities "were constructed by the races who occupied the country at the time of the invasion by the Spaniards, or of some not very distant progenitors."

The travelers ended their trip with an inspection of the deserted city of Uxmal, about 245 miles northeast of Palenque in Yucatan. So great was their enthusiasm that they returned to Yucatan the following year to examine other ruins on the peninsula and the islands offshore, bringing the total number of visited sites to more than 40. Their experiences and findings were published in two illustrated books—*Incidents of Travel in Central America, Chiapas, and Yucatan* and *Incidents of Travel in Yucatan*—that appeared in 1841 and 1843. Readers found them irresistible, and they were immediately translated into many languages; they also had to be reprinted dozens of times to keep up with demand. Almost overnight, the ancient Maya had vaulted from obscurity to celebrity.

But so much about them was still unknown that, for decades to come, imaginative minds could still run wild when contemplating the long-lost cities. As late as the 1880s, for example, many people listened with interest to the theories of a Frenchman named Augustus Le Plongeon, who spent some years in Yucatan and fancied himself a great archaeologist. Among his startling claims were that the hieroglyphs in the ruined cities were a written record of the collapse of the lost continent of Atlantis; bas-reliefs of bearded men at Chichén

PRESERVING THE LEGACY OF CHICHEN ITZA: A DISCERNING EYE FOR DETAIL

"She has a very peculiar character, but most certainly is a true artist," wrote the American consul to Yucatan of the Englishwoman Adela Breton, who at the age of 50 ventured on her own to Chichén Itzá in 1900 to paint its many wonders. And a good thing she did. With the site besieged in the years since by the climate, encroaching jungle, and hordes of visitors, much of Chichén's glory has all but vanished. Today its enchantment is largely remembered through the creations of this independent Victorian whose wanderlust took her to Mexico 13 times between the years 1900 and 1908 before her death, in 1923.

Breton copied the stone carvings, wall paintings, and other artifacts with a passion for accuracy. Although she sometimes produced photographs, they did not meet her exacting standards. "Drawing to scale is the only right method," she proclaimed in a letter, but lamented that "drawing in 1/32 of an inch and correcting to 1/64 is very trying to brain and nerves as well as to eyes and hand." Breton's meticulousness extended to the colors of the frescoes and painted sculpture. Scholars are particularly grateful that she took such pains to record them, because the brilliant hues of the originals have faded dramatically.

Yet despite her rigorous grounding in reality, Breton worked on an intuitive level that breathed life into her subjects: "Making drawings of them would require not modern artistic skill, but the very different capacity of seeing them as ancient Americans did." Indeed, she developed a sort of personal relationship with a group of stone figures unearthed from the Upper Temple of the Jaguars *(inset, opposite),* remarking, "As I lived with them for two months, I felt they were women. They did not approve of me at first—not understanding the modern woman!"

Artist Adela Breton posed sidesaddle for this photograph with her Mexican assistant and friend, Pablo Solorio, upon whose death she mourned, "I shall be like a violinist who has lost the one instrument he can play on."

Rich with detail, Breton's watercolor of the east facade of the Annexe of the Nunnery and the Church at Chichén Itzá, to its right, faithfully re-creates the hooknosed Chac masks and other elaborate Maya motifs sculpted into the stone. In the foreground and atop the buildings, Breton also rendered some of the vegetation that had accumulated over centuries of abandonment.

Adela Breton called her front and rear views (far left) of figures like the one inset at left drawings, which she hastily produced even as officials were carting away this statue and its 14 mates from the Upper Temple of the Jaguars.

Itzá proved that the Phoenicians had visited there; Masonic rites had been carried out at Uxmal 11,500 years ago; and the electric telegraph had been in use among the Maya a few millennia later.

Happily, such notions were gradually overwhelmed by the flood of facts that began pouring in from the Maya homeland. Photographers were publishing images of the ruins as early as the 1860s, and by the 1880s their record of the stone cities was voluminous *(pages 35-45)*. In 1885, the American Antiquarian Society and Harvard's Peabody Museum sent a young scholar named Edward H. Thompson to Yucatan to conduct an extensive archaeological investigation. He spent the next 40 years there, learning the local language so well that he was practically adopted by the Indians. Digging in places that had been ignored by previous visitors, he traced an ancient highway, unearthed evidence of how the lower orders of Maya society had lived, determined that diet had changed little in the region over the centuries, and illuminated many other prosaic but vital matters. In the meantime, the Peabody Museum was sponsoring expeditions by whole teams of specialists. In a series of excavations carried out in Copán between 1891 and 1895, Peabody groups cleared plazas and important structures, mapped the center of the city, and inventoried its monuments. These efforts marked the beginning of truly scientific studies of the Maya, a process that gained momentum in the decades to follow.

Nonetheless, at first only modest headway was made in answering some of the biggest questions about the ancient Maya—questions about their history, their customs, their social and political organization, and the relationships between their cities. John Lloyd Stephens had suspected that many of the answers might be found in the hieroglyphs, which he was confident would someday be deciphered. In fact, some of the ingredients for successful code break-

Pages from the Madrid Codex—one of only four surviving Maya books—are crowded with scores of glyphs. The codex, rescued from oblivion in the 19th century, has proved an invaluable aid in deciphering the Maya script, one of the most complex ever devised by any civilization.

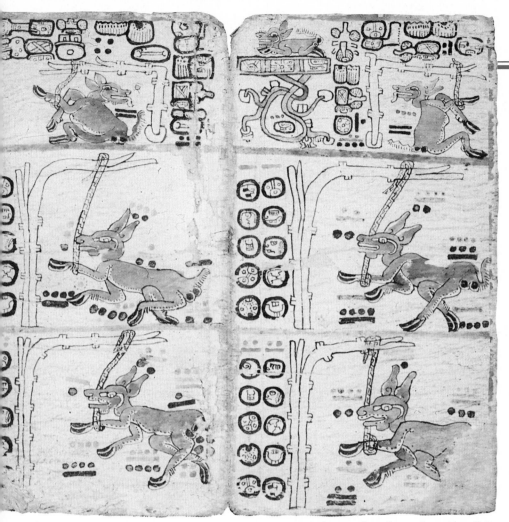

ing were soon to be delivered into scholarly hands. One helpful tool dated from the 16th century, when Spanish friars had taught members of the Indian elite how to write their own languages using the Roman alphabet. At that time, a young noble of the Quiché Maya in Guatemala—who still knew and used the ancient form of writing—transcribed a masterpiece known as the *Popol Vuh* (Book of the community), which was a collection of myths and legends sacred to his people. Unfortunately, the original hieroglyphic version was subsequently lost, but the transcription came to the attention of scholars in the mid-19th century and provided valuable clues to the mind of the ancient Maya. Researchers also found a set of Spanish-era manuscripts from Yucatan that had also been rewritten with Roman letters. Known as the *Books of Chilam Balam*—a reference to an order of "Jaguar Priests"—they dealt principally with folklore, calendrical matters, and medicine.

Scholars were grateful for the cultural information contained in these documents, but the manuscripts were also a painful reminder of the literary riches that had disappeared. When the Spaniards first arrived, the Maya had probably possessed thousands of books written in hieroglyphs on bark paper, just like those that Landa had consigned to the flames. Only a minuscule fraction of this great body of literature escaped similar destruction, passing through various hands as curiosities and fetching up in libraries and collections. In the 19th century, scholars knew of only three such texts—the so-called codices—and each was named for the city where it came to light: the Dresden Codex, the Paris Codex, and the Madrid Codex. (Fragments of a fourth, the Grolier Codex, have since been discovered.) The first of these would significantly advance the cause of comprehending the ancient Maya. Studying it over a 14-year period beginning in 1880, the head librarian of the Royal Library in Dresden, Ernst Forste-

HIEROGLYPHS: COMPACT REPOSITORIES OF TIME, PEOPLE, DEEDS, AND GLORY

Maya hieroglyphs look like miniature works of art crammed into small squares; in fact, they are precise units of writing in a complex script, one of only five known independently created systems of written language. Their pictorial quality allowed those familiar with the symbols to read them without much training and gave scribes scope to display their skills and creativity.

Some glyphs represent consonant-plus-vowel syllables. Most, however, are ideographs—signs for phrases, words, or parts of words. Glyph blocks are often composed of a main sign with affixes used to reinforce the beginning sound of a word.

Glyphs are found carved on steles, door lintels, and stairway risers, and also painted on codices, pottery, and tomb walls. Some 800 have been identified, and new decipherments—and reinterpretations of old ones—mount as interest grows.

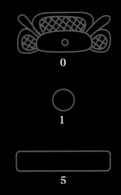

The above three symbols were used to form all numbers. Here, the top glyph stands for 0; the dot, 1; the bar, 5. Two bars and a dot represent 11.

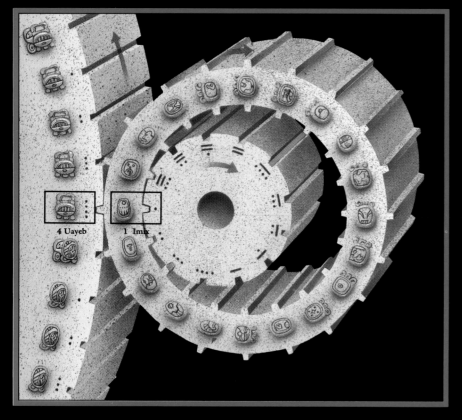

4 Uayeb   1 Imix

In the schematic diagram (left), gears illustrate the interaction of the two Maya calendars, which bear glyphs deciphered by Landa in 1566, and give the date as 1 Imix 4 Uayeb (read from right to left). The largest gear represents the 365-day solar calendar of eighteen 20-day months with five extra days, a period called Uayeb, "the sleep." The two smaller gears indicate the 260-day Sacred Almanac of twenty 13-day months. The larger gear displays the 20 day names, while the smaller one shows day numbers up to 13. When a day name and number repeated themselves, the Sacred Almanac had completed its 260-day revolution. But it took 52 years for the combination of 1 Imix in the Sacred Almanac and 4 Uayeb in the solar calendar to overlap.

BALAM

BA-BALAM

BA-LA-M(A)

To Battle

Lord of Copán

The signs above are examples of two types of glyphs. The so-called event glyph (above, left) is thought to refer to a military event, as is suggested by the ax, and reads as the verb "to battle." The emblem glyph (above, right) names an individual as supreme ruler of a domain or people. In this glyph—translated "Lord of Copán"—the main sign is a bat's head, possibly signifying that the ruler is chief of the bat tribe.

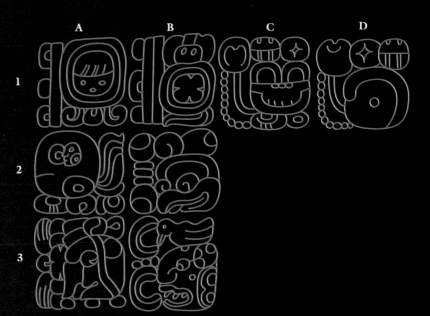

A B C D

1
2
3

Maya writing often combines ideographs with phonetic syllables to enhance the significance of a word. For example, the word balam, *meaning jaguar, is shown above as it appears in Maya writing. The top glyph is the ideograph for jaguar. An affix representing the syllable* ba *is attached to the middle symbol. On the bottom, the word* jaguar *is written only in syllabic signs, reading clockwise from far left to right,* ba la ma. *Since final vowels are never pronounced, it would be read as "balam."*

Maya glyphs, like those above, are read downward, left to right, in pairs. Typically, texts began with a calendar date, followed by an event glyph explaining what happened on that date and then the name and titles of the ruler involved. This text reads: On 6 Imix (A1) 12 Yaxkin (B1) was seated on the throne (A2), captor of (B2) Lord Hok of Palenque (A3), Bird Jaguar of Yaxchilan (B3), Sovereign Lord of Yaxchilan (C1 and C2). The glyphs are accurate, but the text has been fabricated, using Maya style and syntax, for purposes of illustration.

31

mann, was able to figure out the mechanics of the Maya calendar.

In his efforts to fathom the mysteries of Maya timekeeping, Forstemann made extensive use of another manuscript that had been found and published about two decades earlier—not a Maya document, but one infamous observer's sincere attempt to describe their world. This was the treatise composed by Landa in the 1560s as he awaited judgment in Spain for his brutal methods of weaning the Indians from their religious beliefs. A copy of the fact-filled report had lain buried in the Academy of History in Madrid for centuries.

Its discoverer was a French cleric, Abbé Charles Etienne Brasseur de Bourbourg, a former journalist and novelist who became a priest at the age of 31. After taking holy orders, Brasseur de Bourbourg spent time in the United States, Canada, Italy, and then Mexico, where he finally found his true calling—the study of Mesoamerican cultures through old documents. He learned several Indian languages, became a confidant of numerous scholars and collectors, and managed, between 1846 and 1869, to track down scores of precious texts. In the field of Maya studies, the three most important of his finds were a copy of Landa's description of the native culture in Yucatan; part of a huge dictionary of Maya words compiled by a Franciscan friar in the 16th century (Brasseur de Bourbourg chanced upon it in a secondhand bookstore in Mexico City); and a portion of the Madrid Codex. Brasseur de Bourbourg also published an important translation of the *Popol Vuh*—and always claimed credit for unearthing this work as well. Actually, a German physician had beat him to it, spotting it in a Guatemalan library in 1854.

Russian linguist Yuri Knorosov, whose articles, published in the 1950s, revolutionized Maya studies, exhibits an even more baleful look than his cat. Knorosov proposed correctly that the Maya could have used, in addition to pictographs, glyphs as purely phonetic syllables. But because his papers were marked by Marxist-Leninist cant and some of his conclusions were faulty, Western scholars were slow to accept his theory.

Without question, however, Brasseur de Bourbourg's most important contribution was his rediscovery of Landa's journal—the single richest source of information about Maya culture ever to come into scholarly possession. The most critical section turned out to be the account of Landa's own attempt to find the meaning of the hieroglyphs. That day when he sat with an Indian who could still write in the age-old Maya way, he compiled a set of 27 or so glyphs that he took to be phonetic equivalents of various sounds represented by letters in the Spanish alphabet. (In alphabetic writing, each letter stands for a basic phonetic building block of a spoken language.) Unfortunately, these symbols proved almost worthless when modern-day researchers tried to use them in translating the codices or the inscriptions on steles and elsewhere in the stone cities. As a result, many scholars concluded that Landa had been on a completely wrong track and that Maya writing was ideographic; that is, that the glyphs represented concepts rather than sounds.

The few symbols successfully deciphered after the discovery of the Landa manuscript were designations for numbers, dating methods, astronomical cycles, and the like—which led many experts to conclude that Maya writing was limited to such matters. As late as the 1950s this was still the most prevalent view, and its chief spokesmen were the American archaeologist Sylvanus G. Morley of the Carnegie Institution in Washington, D.C., and J. Eric S. Thompson, a British archaeologist also affiliated with Carnegie. Thompson drew a picture of the Maya as a peaceful, contemplative people, obsessed with the passage of time, and guided by priests who watched the movements of celestial bodies and discerned in them the will of the gods. Maya cities were ceremonial centers, he believed, not bastions of worldly power. "The great theme of Maya civilization," he wrote in 1956, "is the passage of time—the wide concept of the mystery of eternity and the narrower concept of the divisions of time into their equivalents of centuries, years, months, and days. The rhythm of time enchanted the Maya; the never-ending flow of days from the eternity of the future into the eternity of the past filled them with wonder."

As long as no one could read the vast majority of the hieroglyphs, there was little basis for challenging this portrait. But in 1952, a little-known Soviet linguist named Yuri Knorosov began to reshape the accepted thinking. Knorosov, an expert on Egyptian hieroglyphs, had become interested in the signs that made up what Landa thought was the Maya alphabet. He examined the various surviving codices and found that, collectively, they contained approximately 300 distinct glyphs. If all the signs were ideograms, this number was strangely small. On the other hand, a phonetic system—using either an alphabet (the smallest units of sound) or syllabic units (a vowel plus a consonant)—would have far fewer signs. Knorosov postulated that Maya writing was a hybrid system, part phonetic and part semantic—as was the case with many early scripts, including those of ancient Mesopotamia, Egypt, and China. He went on to show that, in its phonetic aspect, Maya writing was based on syllables rather than on alphabetic letters. He guessed that Landa's informant had actually used consonant-vowel combinations to represent Spanish letters: For example, when Landa pronounced the letter "l," his

Siberian-born archaeologist Tatiana Proskouriakoff examines Maya jade fragments in her basement office at Harvard's Peabody Museum. Making a breakthrough in the deciphering of Maya glyphs in the 1960s parallel to Knorosov's, she also transformed Maya scholarship by showing that most inscriptions concern dynastic history, telling of the births, deaths, and deeds of rulers and nobles. Trained originally as an architect, she was known too for her beautiful and correct renderings of Maya ruins.

Indian partner would have drawn the sign for the syllable "lu."

Many scholars disputed Knorosov's ideas at first, and some of his assertions were indeed proven wrong. Moreover, the script itself, once deciphered, presented numerous difficulties: Maya syntax and grammar, as other scholars would eventually demonstrate, were idiosyncratic; phonetic and ideographic elements were often blended; glyphs appeared in different styles; and the texts were riddled with puns, metaphors, and obscure allusions. Because of these complexities and the flaws in Knorosov's papers, the phonetic dimension of Maya writing was not widely accepted until the early 1970s.

By then, two other breakthroughs had occurred. In 1958 Heinrich Berlin, an epigrapher who had spent years examining panels at Palenque and other Maya centers in the southern lowlands, noted a similarity in certain blocks of glyphs at widely scattered sites: These blocks had distinctive main signs but a single type of prefix—a similar context, in effect. Berlin surmised that the distinctive main glyph was either a placename or the name of the family that had ruled the city. He called these signs emblem glyphs. They were the first clear indication that Maya writing was not exclusively concerned with priestly wisdom about time and the heavens.

In 1960 Tatiana Proskouriakoff, a Russian-born colleague of Eric Thompson's at the Carnegie Institution, secured the case for worldly content in the hieroglyphic texts. Examining a number of steles at Piedras Negras, a ruined Maya city about 60 miles southeast of Palenque, she discerned patterns of dates associated with glyphs that looked as if they might represent important events. Over and over again, the dates seemed to mark off a human lifespan, ranging in length from 56 to 64 years. Sets of dates often overlapped, and they were linked to portraits of women, children, and young Maya lords. She concluded that the monuments recorded key happenings in the lives of the city's dynastic rulers—births, accessions to power, triumphs in war, deaths, and so on. The evidence was indisputable. The Maya had recorded their history in stone.

The insights of Knorosov, Berlin, and Proskouriakoff launched a new age in Maya studies. Since then, upward of 80 percent of Maya glyphs have surrendered their meaning, and a fresh generation of archaeologists has been inspired to dig deeper and learn more. As a result, the entire Maya world has begun to come into focus, glorious not just in its art and its architecture but in the full scope of its humanity and its history.

To a curious 19th-century world, photographs of the splendid ruins of ancient Maya cities were almost as good as seeing them firsthand. Today, the images continue to exert their pull. The extraordinary clarity and detail of the pictures, however, give little hint of the formidable effort behind them. The photography of the time, requiring bulky cameras, fragile glass negatives, and copious supplies of chemicals, was greatly complicated by the primitive conditions and difficult transportation in Maya country. "It would be well to have a full gross of plates ordered," wrote Edward H. Thompson in 1888 to a trustee of Harvard's Peabody Museum, which had funded his expedition, "as a certain percentage of damaged and broken plates is always to be expected, especially in this hot, damp, mule-packing land."

The quality of the pictures that emerged from the rain forest testified to the dedication of the photographers—mostly gentleman adventurers with little tech-

nical training. One of the most prominent was Alfred Maudslay, whose photographs at Chichén Itzá included the huge serpent head at the main pyramid, El Castillo *(detail, above)*. A former British colonial administrator, Maudslay came to Central America in 1881 out of "a desire to pass the winter in a warm climate," as he later wrote. "However, the interest awakened by the sight of the truly wonderful monuments induced me to undertake other expeditions."

Those expeditions continued for 13 years, all eight paid for out of his own pocket. In addition to a wealth of photographs, Maudslay took more than a thousand casts from Maya steles and other monuments, and produced drawings and plans of several important sites that would fill eight volumes—four of text and four of illustrations. The record left by Maudslay and his contemporaries still contributes to Maya research; in some cases their photographs are the only remaining record of carvings since destroyed or eroded away.

PAVING THE WAY FOR THE SCHOLARS

Alfred Maudslay visited more than a dozen Maya sites, focusing his efforts on such major cities as Copán, Quiriguá, Palenque, and Tikal. He worked among the ruins for most of eight dry seasons, spending the rainy months collating his material and writing up his finds.

The rain forest slowed fieldwork with debilitating fevers and formidable insects that were sometimes more than a nuisance: When a phalanx of army ants invaded a camp at Copán, it consumed everything edible in its path, including, as he pointed out, "the films of two recently developed photographs left in the rack to dry." Maudslay was determined to overcome such obstacles; his goal was to collect materials that would let scholars "solve the problems of the Maya civilization whilst comfortably seated at home in their studies."

Maudslay shot the north face of the tower at Palenque in 1891, soon after the area in front of it had been cleared. When he first saw the ruin, it was, he noted, "almost filled to the level of the floors" with broken masonry that had fallen from the building. The debris was disposed of "by throwing it down the outside slope of the foundation mound," a method that horrifies today's archaeologists.

PIECING TOGETHER THE PAST

The Austrian photographer and explorer Teobert Maler traveled to Mexico in 1865 to join the army of the ill-fated Emperor Maximilian and remained there several years. Called back home, he spent time in Austria, France, and England, but returned to Mexico in 1884 when his interest was piqued by stories of the archaeological finds being made there. His plan was to produce a photographic atlas of the ruins, to be sold by subscription. The book never materialized, but he was hired by the Peabody Museum in 1897 and produced photographs for it over a 10-year period that were included in major reports on several previously unstudied sites. Not only did he record many important sites and monuments, taking measurements of them as well as pictures, but he also pioneered the art of photo-

To give this photograph scale, Maler had a worker pose with a fallen stele at Piedras Negras, in Guatemala. He preferred flexible film to glass plates, which broke easily during transport in the jungle.

PRESENTING THE MAYA TO THE WORLD

osted to Yucatan and Campeche as American consul in 1885, primarily to conduct archaeological studies at Labná and Uxmal, Edward H. Thompson spent much of his time exploring ruins. His work gained popular attention through a huge display of photographs and architectural castings at the Columbian Exposition in Chicago in 1893.

CAPTURING STONE ON PAPER

arvard's Peabody Museum mounted four large-scale expeditions to Copán between 1891 and 1895. When the director of the second expedition, John Owens, died of a tropical fever in 1893, Maudslay briefly took over, interrupting his honeymoon to do so. One goal was to take casts of the monuments, since removing them from their jungle setting and shipping them home would have been all but impossible.

Mounted on a mule (above), John Owens of the Peabody Museum is the very picture of an expedition leader. Porters, rather than mules, were entrusted with transporting bundled papier-mâché casts.

Tumbled into ruins by time, a giant stele at Copán (left) displays rich detail. The subsequent weathering of such monuments renders a photograph like this one by Maudslay an invaluable record.

GODS, BLOOD, AND KINGS

Believed to be the portrait of a now-forgotten ruler of Cuello, this three-inch-high pottery head wears the trappings of early Maya royalty—ear ornaments and a simple diadem. The figure was made around 400 BC, a time when most Maya lived in small farming and trading villages.

For a moment or two, the British archaeologist Norman Hammond stared unrecognizing at the smooth round object that lay before him amid the rubble of a temple courtyard at Cuello, a relatively unknown Maya site in northern Belize. But then, in a flash, he realized what it was: the back of a human skull, its face still buried in the soil. As Hammond and his team of excavators began to dig, they came upon other human remains in the same small area—some complete skeletons, others with hacked-off skulls and limbs. The final tally indicated that more than 30 people had been buried here, and although many of the skeletons were badly crushed by the debris that had piled up over them in the intervening centuries, there could be little doubt that this was no ordinary grave site.

One skull bore a neat hole in the forehead that was a perfect fit for one of the ceremonial daggers—chiseled from a kind of flint known as chert—that the team was also turning up. All of the bones had been found within a circular depression at the hub of a raised area that apparently had been erected around and over them. Two young men had been placed with their heads almost touching, their feet pointing apart, and a number of pottery vessels arranged around them. More bones from severed arms and legs had then been scattered over this centerpiece, and to complete the grisly tableau, bodies had been propped in a seated position around the circle. Clearly this had been a scene of sacrifice, with the victims most likely slaughtered to dedicate the building of a new temple complex.

For Hammond and his colleagues, whose excavations of Cuello had begun in 1976 and continued into the 1990s, it was a thrilling discovery—the first direct physical evidence of mass human sacrifice by the Maya. Only a generation earlier, leading scholars had maintained that the Maya were little interested in violence and bloodshed, even of a ritual nature. In 1915, the American archaeologist Sylvanus G. Morley had noted depictions of warfare in Maya carvings, but he essentially ignored them; during later studies, he concentrated instead on the dating schemes and knowledge of celestial phenomena he discerned in the glyphs, leaving out of his drawings the pictorial representations he had seen of less sophisticated pursuits—what he referred to as textual residue. He was, it seems, intent on demonstrating that the Maya were "the Greeks of the New World," a civilization whose intellectual attainments made them "the greatest race that ever lived on this earth."

But while there is no denying Maya achievements in mathematics or astronomy, here at Cuello was irrefutable proof of their obsession with the spilling of blood—their own as well as that of sacrificial victims presumably taken from the ranks of captured enemies. For in addition to the many items recovered from the site that testified to mortal sacrifice was a stingray spine, which pictographs suggest was used in ritual ceremony by men to draw blood from their earlobes or penises and by women from their tongues.

What made the cluster of bodies at Cuello particularly significant was the apparent date of their burial, at a time that marked a historical watershed in the development of Maya civilization. Analysis of the site's various layers suggested that the victims had been sacrificed around 400 BC, when lowland peoples in the region now comprising southern Yu-

The scattered bones of 32 people sacrificed at Cuello 2,400 years ago include the skull of a young man killed by a sharp dagger thrust to the forehead. A blade made of chert that was found nearby fit the wound as snugly as a knife in its sheath. A similar chert weapon (below) was recovered from a nearby Cuello burial. The victims were probably warriors captured from a neighboring community.

catan, Guatemala, and Belize were beginning to transform their farming and trading villages into ceremonial centers that would eventually grow into complex and sophisticated cities. Piecing together what had happened at Cuello, Hammond and his fellow investigators deduced that the inhabitants had converted their existing ceremonial precinct—a courtyard surrounded by wood-and-thatch temples—into a massive public arena. After burning the temples and ripping apart their facades in a rite of deconsecration, the villagers had filled in the square with rubble, creating a raised platform of more than an acre. It was at the center of this structure that the sacrificial victims—almost all young and possibly all male—were interred.

Buried with them were six tubes made of carved bone, thought by some to be nothing more than ceremonial fan holders but by others to be the handles of bloodletting instruments. But more important than their function was the design etched into four of them, an interlacing pattern identifiable as the Maya *pop,* or woven mat. Evidence at other, later sites indicated that such mats were used by Maya kings and were the iconographic equivalent of thrones. Their discovery at Cuello suggested that by 400 BC—far earlier than most experts had expected—Maya society may have been dominated, both symbolically and in reality, by a royal elite.

In fact, at this small and ancient site, one of hundreds throughout Maya territory dating to the same era, Hammond's team was finding many precursors of Maya culture that eventually would evolve into the defining features of the civilization at its height. Digging into a small pyramid at the western end of the platform, they found another pyramid within, which had served, in typical Maya fashion, as the foundation for the later structure. The interior building was adorned with enigmatic designs, each framed by an oval ring. To Hammond they looked remarkably like later Maya hieroglyphic characters, suggesting that the Cuello villagers had already acquired the basic elements of Maya writing even if they had yet to develop them into a functional system. These people were probably numerate as well. From a tomb inside the pyramid Hammond recovered several seals, one of which was inscribed with a vertical bar and four dots: the Maya symbol for the number 9.

To top it all off, in front of the pyramid the team came upon an unusual chunk of limestone. Hammond took little notice of it at first, regarding it as a "natural nuisance," but one morning, seeing it from the top of the pyramid, he realized that it had been squared off by hand and was most likely a stele, one of the stone slabs on which the Maya carved inscriptions and images of their rulers. Until then, the earliest known stele was at Tikal, in Guatemala. Dated to AD 292, it has traditionally been used to mark the beginning of what is known as the Classic period—a span of 600 years during which Maya civilization reached its peak and such commemoration of kings and their achievements was common. Here at Cuello, though, was a monument apparently fulfilling a similar function but estimated to have been erected more than 200 years earlier.

And there were even older archaeological treasures awaiting. As part of an earlier investigation not long after Hammond first spotted the site in 1973, researchers had dug a test pit deep into the soil at Cuello, pulling up samples of burned wood from what they assumed were the earliest phases of occupation. Radiocarbon dating of these samples suggested that people had lived there as far

back as around 1000 BC and perhaps even earlier, when the first farming villages were beginning to be established throughout the region. The findings spoke to a longstanding debate about the genesis of Maya civilization. Some experts argued that the origins must be sought in ancient Mexico, while others claimed that the roots lay in the highlands of Central America; still others postulated a link with Chinese or Southeast Asian civilizations. But if it could be shown that the earliest inhabitants of Cuello were direct ancestors of the Maya, it would indicate that the Maya were the makers of their own history, rather than mere borrowers or adapters.

Stratified remains of civic remodeling projects dating back to 2200 BC make up the acre-square, 12-foot-high platform on which the outermost stepped pyramid at Cuello was constructed in 400 BC. Believing that supernatural power accumulated in sacred locales over the years, the Maya continually razed urban centers and rebuilt on top of the ruins.

Armed with the information obtained from radiocarbon dating, Hammond and his team set out to test this speculation, working back through Cuello's history by removing successive floor levels in the main courtyard—the best place to trace the record of occupation—until they reached the remains of the earliest building in the sequence. It had been a hut similar to the pole-framed, palm-thatched houses in which the local Indians, descendants of the Maya, now lived. The structure had been built on a plaster platform—the earliest known use of the lime-plastering technique that was such a feature of architecture during the Maya heyday.

The different levels of the courtyard provided striking evidence of the continuity of a cultural tradition at Cuello. First laid out late in the second millennium BC, it maintained the same basic floor plan through the centuries, growing higher and grander until the day when it was filled in with rubble and commemorated by human sacrifice. At one edge of the platform the archaeologists discovered a cistern, originally used as a storage vault but converted sometime around the first or second century AD into a rubbish dump. From it they recovered kernels of corn, the staple of the Maya diet throughout their history. Comparing these seeds with earlier specimens, experts found signs of genetic improvements apparently made by succeeding generations of Maya farmers. Indeed, Hammond reckoned that at Cuello yields had more than doubled between the village's founding and the year AD 200.

Further discoveries revealed that from the beginning the vil-

lagers of Cuello were making competent pottery in a range of colors, and by the seventh century BC they were decorating it with resin and firing the clay to produce a permanent design. One bowl from this period depicts a water bird; another fragment dating from about 1,000 years later is incised with an image of what appears to be a topknot—a hairstyle that recurs in later Maya art. Another pottery artifact dating from around 1000 BC proved to be a child's whistle in the shape of a bird with four holes in its side. Not long after finding it, Hammond—unable to resist—blew through the mouthpiece and, fingering the holes, produced the five notes of the diatonic scale, a timeless and universal sequence that must have been as familiar to the inhabitants of the ancient New World as it was to him.

A two-inch-long terra-cotta stamp made ca. AD 100 bears the four dots and single vertical bar that designated the number 9 in Maya. Such stamps were probably used to print designs on skin or textiles.

This especially evocative item was found in the grave of a child of about six and was part of a cache of goods that included a piece of jade—an extremely hard mineral that was greatly valued in Meso-america. One of its few known sources in the area, rediscovered as recently as 1952, is the valley of the Motagua River in southern Guatemala. It was apparently from here that the ancient Olmec of Mexico's Gulf Coast, a mysterious people who rose to prominence at least 500 years before the Maya, obtained the raw stones that they fashioned into ceremonial objects and jewelry of high quality. According to Hammond, an exchange of trade goods between the Olmec and the first inhabitants of Cuello, 400 miles to the east, is possible, suggesting that from early on the two groups influenced each other's cultural development. Other scholars are less certain, pointing out that items might have been exchanged through inter-mediaries, and that no firm evidence of such influence exists.

A bowl recovered from a Cuello burial site dating from 250 BC testifies to the artistry of the community's craftspeople. The smooth orange glaze and the incised design around the rim of the vessel are both typical of Cuello pottery, among the oldest found in Central America.

In the Classic period, great Maya rulers were accompanied to their graves by lavish strands of jade or inlaid masks; but as the graves at Cuello revealed, the practice of placing jade with the dead had begun more than a millennium earlier. Even at this ancient date there are signs that the Maya distinguished between different qualities of jade, valuing above all others stones of a translucent emerald green that resembled the iridescent hues of the quetzal, a bird native to the Maya highlands whose feathers were highly prized for human adornment. Tiny beads of this precious jade were recovered from a few of the 172 Cuello burials ultimately excavated by Hammond, who found that people of low status were sometimes interred with artifacts made from less-valued minerals that resembled jade only in color.

For the Maya, jade's worth went beyond its purely decorative appeal. Its color symbolized life itself—the green of growing corn, the glimmering shades of deep pools of water. In the Maya lexicon, the hieroglyph for jade was also used as a day name that represented rain, and according to a ritual text in use at the time of the Spanish conquest, jade was "the precious stone of grace, the first infinite grace." In addition, it was metaphorically linked with blood, the symbol of life and of death. Blood shed by kings in sacred rituals fertilized the great tree *(axis mundi)* at the center of the Maya universe and also opened the doorway into a parallel world of supernatural beings whose actions influenced the everyday world. Small wonder then that the Maya decorated many of their jade pieces with red pigments, thus symbolically uniting the two most profoundly important elements of their world.

On the last day of his excavations at Cuello, Norman Hammond climbed down to an ancient hearth set in the lowest layer of the site and, in thanks for the successful conclusion of the project, burned an offering of *pom,* a resin incense still used by modern Maya in religious rituals. Looking up at the sequence of structures he had uncovered, he felt sure that his hypothesis had been correct: The Maya, though perhaps stimulated by neighboring cultures such as the Olmec, had shaped their own destiny. This one small site contained all the ingredients necessary for the evolution of a complex society—fine crafts, the rudiments of mathematics and literacy, a progressive approach to agriculture indicated by genetic improvements in corn, widespread trading links, a hierarchical organization. What was missing, though, was a clue to the impetus that finally propelled Maya society from a thriving village culture into an urban civilization.

Some 10 years later, at an obscure site in the tropical forest of

Only two inches long from nose to tail, a tiny bird-shaped ocarina found in the grave of a Cuello child still sounds the do-re-mi-fa-sol tones of the diatonic scale through its air vents.

Archaeologists in 1980 struggle through a swamp in the Maya lowlands on their 40-mile-long hike to the remote ruins of El Mirador. Discovered in 1926, the metropolis where the Maya constructed some of their largest public buildings was virtually inaccessible until 1972, when an airstrip—later overgrown by jungle—was laid out near the site.

northern Guatemala, the archaeologist Richard Hansen of the University of California at Los Angeles (UCLA) thought he had found the answer. Rediscovered in 1930 by aerial reconnaissance but not visited by archaeologists until 1962, the ruins lie about 215 miles from Guatemala City and eight and a half miles from the six-square-mile Maya metropolis of El Mirador, which had been ranked as the earliest Maya city, dating from the second century BC. An ancient causeway had once linked the two settlements, and for this reason, the new site had been given the name Nakbé, which in Yucatec Maya means "by the road." When Hansen made his first foray there in 1987, he had to hack his way across a formidable swamp, relying on compass bearings taken from pyramids at El Mirador to find his way across the dense jungle. Two years later, a train of 125 mules made the same journey, carrying the equipment of a joint expedition organized by the Guatemalan Institute of Anthropology and History and UCLA.

As it turned out, Nakbé was thriving some centuries before El Mirador, and its foundations went back nearly 3,000 years. Although some finds at Cuello may have been more ancient, Nakbé had obviously been a much grander place, complete with a ceremonial center more than half a mile across, with massive platforms and 150-foot-high pyramids built about 300 BC and smaller 60-foot pyramids as long ago as 600 BC, when Cuello and many other sites were still simple villages. Here, too, the different layers of the settlement produced a picture of a society that had grown more and more complex. Decorative seashells and obsidian tools that had been imported suggested to Hansen that the people of Nakbé had early on developed well-organized systems for procuring and transporting various goods. The discovery of human teeth inlaid with jadelike stone, a form of dental ornamentation common among the elite in Classic Maya times, served as evidence that a social hierarchy existed in Nakbé perhaps as early as 2,800 years ago. A fragment of pottery from the same period bore the image of a human profile with a characteristic sloping forehead—a badge of high status among later Maya, who had deliberately bound the skulls of newborns to produce the effect, which the Maya scholar John

Carlson believes was intended to give their heads the shape of an ear of corn, making them "men of maize."

As at Cuello, the inhabitants of Nakbé embarked on an extensive construction program between 2,400 and 2,600 years ago, burying their early ceremonial structures under huge platforms on which they erected pyramids and other structures. Initially, the facades were left blank, but around 300 BC large decorative stucco panels were added to some of the upper surfaces, depicting monsters with exaggerated features. These masks had been painstakingly carved into the underlying limestone before stucco was applied, whereas at other sites the artists had saved time and effort by building up the masks from the stucco itself. To Hansen, this suggested that the facades at Nakbé were possibly among the oldest ever discovered in the Maya lowlands.

Even at this early date, ceremonial structures conformed to a standard pattern. Pyramids at Nakbé and other nearby sites were

An artist sketches the stone mask of a mythological deity as it is uncovered on a pyramid at El Mirador. Starting around 300 BC, the emerging Maya elite began using elaborately stuccoed stone reliefs on the facades of their temples to promulgate a political and religious doctrine in which rulers were seen as communicating directly with the gods.

crowned with three small temples clustered at the top of an upper stairway flanked by panels and masks. The upper stairway at Nakbé's main pyramid had 13 steps, probably corresponding to the 13 levels of the Maya heavens, each of which was associated with its own god.

In one respect, however, the public architecture at Nakbé differed from that in later Maya cities, which bristled with steles bearing images and hieroglyphs that glorified the lives and achievements of their rulers. At Nakbé the ornamental depictions focused instead on gods and creatures from mythology. One of the center's most extraordinary artworks was a scene that appeared in duplicate on both sides of an 11-foot-high limestone stele that had been smashed to bits—apparently on purpose but for unknown reasons—much later in Nakbé's history. Carefully reassembling the fragments, Hansen was able to make out two figures in royal garb, one of whom was pointing to a disembodied head that seemed to be loosely connected to the other's headdress. After studying the images, Hansen felt sure that they represented characters from the *Popol Vuh,* the famous Maya epic that had been transcribed from its hieroglyphic original and translated into Spanish sometime in the 16th century.

Thought by some scholars to have been formulated around the time that Nakbé was undergoing its transformation, the epic features the so-called Hero Twins, Hunahpu and Xbalanque, whose father—named Hun Hunahpu—had been a twin as well. The story tells of how Hun Hunahpu and his brother are tortured and beheaded after losing a ball game to the Lords of the Underworld, known as Xibalba, the Place of Fright. Summoned in turn to the Underworld, the Hero Twins manage to defeat the Xibalbans and later ascend to glory, transformed into the sun and the moon. According to Hansen, the figures on the Nakbé stele appear to be none other than Xbalanque and Hunahpu, and the severed head that of their

HEROES IN THE PLACE OF FRIGHT

"This is the account of how all was in suspense, all calm, in silence; all motionless, and the expanse of the sky was empty." Thus begins the *Popol Vuh,* the Maya story of creation. Among the lively characters peopling it are two sets of brothers, who are avid ballplayers. The first pair, Hun Hunahpu and Vucub Hunahpu, are summoned to Xibalba, the Place of Fright, or Underworld, by its two rulers who covet their sporting gear and intend to steal it. The harassed brothers wind up being tortured and put to death. Hun Hunahpu's corpse is decapitated and his head hung on a barren calabash tree that instantly bears fruit. "Let no one come to pick this fruit," the rulers command. But a young woman, drawn to the tree, plucks a gourd. As she does so, Hun Hunahpu's head, now reduced to a skull, dribbles spittle into her palm, causing her to become pregnant. Leaving the Underworld, she goes to live in the house of Hun Hunahpu's mother and there gives birth to twin boys, Hunahpu and Xbalanque.

Like Hun Hunahpu and his brother, the twins are summoned to Xibalba to participate in a ball game. Cleverer by far than their father and uncle, they manage to avoid the tortures and pitfalls intended for them and defeat their antagonists roundly. But victory does not assure their release. Having angered the men of Xibalba, they undergo various hair-raising experiences; then, using magic, they let themselves be murdered. The Xibalbans grind the twins' bones to powder and toss the remains into a river. "But the bones did not go very far," the *Popol Vuh* relates, "for settling themselves down at once on the bottom of the river, they were changed back into handsome boys."

Returning to Xibalba in disguise, the twins perform a series of tricks—including one sacrificing and then resurrecting the other. Entranced, the two Lords of Xibalba ask for similar treatment, and the twins consent—up to a point: They dispatch the duped leaders but do not bring them back to life. Having vanquished evil, the Hero Twins—as they came to be called—ascend into the sky, where they take up positions as the sun and the moon.

As related in the Popol Vuh, *the slain Hun Hunahpu—regarded by the Maya as the corn god—rises from a split turtle shell representing the earth's surface. He is resurrected by his sons, Hunahpu (left) and Xbalanque (right), as they pour water on the sprouting grain.*

unfortunate father, shown appropriately linked to his namesake son.

Early in 1992, Hansen made an even more exciting discovery at Nakbé, where he and his fellow archaeologists were conducting further excavations of some of the site's hundreds of structures. Clearing the vegetation and soil from the base of a 150-foot-tall pyramid, they began to uncover what would prove to be the largest architectural sculpture ever found in the Maya region. More than 30 feet long and 16 feet high, the giant relief was a stylized head of the Maya god known as the Celestial Bird, an early symbol of the untamed natural world, which in *Popol Vuh* stories had been brought under control by the Hero Twins. Since a Maya king was taken to be the earthly embodiment of the twins, the Celestial Bird later became associated with regal authority and was often depicted presiding over coronations. The most fascinating aspect of the sculpture was that it dated to such an early phase of Maya history—about 300 BC, making it 200 years older than other similar works. To Hansen, this suggested an intriguing possibility: Perhaps the development of a religious ideology had itself served as the spark that ignited the bright flame of Maya civilization.

Throughout his investigations, Hansen had pondered why, suddenly, the people of Nakbé had embarked on a building program of such unparalleled scale. Although the monumental edifices served no apparent practical purpose—except, perhaps, to help channel and collect rainwater in preparation for the four-month dry season—their construction had clearly required a massive effort, with most if not all of the population involved. Only a powerful ruling class or group could have marshaled such a labor force, but the question was how they had managed it. Later on, when hereditary dynasties were well established, buildings were raised in honor of specific rulers, suggesting that the inherent authority of kingship had been sufficient motivation for the masses. But in these early days, those who commissioned monuments dedicated them to supernatural beings. Taking these factors into account, Hansen concluded that the political organization at Nakbé and other sites had a religious foundation, with its leaders and lords—perhaps drawn from the ranks of a priesthood—mobilizing their subjects by appealing to their reverence for the gods.

Other archaeologists have challenged Hansen's claim that religion was the key factor that spurred the development of this complex society. His speculations may in time need revising in the face of more extensive field studies in the area. In any case, at Nakbé the building boom did not last for long. Within a few generations of the time when the bird sculpture had been fashioned, construction came to a virtual halt, and the city soon became little better than a ghost town, remaining that way for close to 1,000 years. Hansen believes that Nakbé gave way to nearby El Mirador, which was blessed with more reliable water sources and better defenses in the form of a steep natural escarpment along its northern and western boundaries.

Whatever the catalyst had been for the rise of Maya civilization, to survive and prosper it had to be sustained by economic resources, including enough food to support a growing class of nonfarmers—ruling families and their households, warriors, and craftspeople. Until the 1960s, the general assumption was that the ancient Maya, like their modern descendants, had depended for almost all of their food on slash-and-burn agriculture, a system that involves clearing fields from the forest and burning the brush to fertilize the ground with ash. Because tropical soil is relatively poor and thin to begin with, the nutrients in such fields are used up quickly, within a year or two, after which the land must lie fallow until new forest vegetation grows back, renewing the soil and enabling farmers to move in again. Researchers have calculated that as a result, less than a third of the land available to the Maya would have been productive in any year, so slash-and-burn agriculture could not possibly have supported large numbers of people dwelling in cities.

For this reason, scholars had speculated that huge sites such as El Mirador must have been primarily ceremonial, occupied by a priestly ruling class and visited by farming families from outlying districts only on special occasions. Even so, evidence suggested that by as early as AD 300, the population had grown to a point that would have stretched a purely slash-and-burn system to its limits. Given that the population would increase tenfold in the next 600 years, the only possibility is that Maya farmers had developed a variety of agricultural methods.

One practice that helped combat erosion—a major problem where slash-and-burn agriculture took place—was the terracing of hillsides, which trapped soil and built it up into thicker, richer layers. The Maya also appear to have supplemented their food supplies with small-scale kitchen gardens and orchards near their homes, where

The 34-foot-wide avian head known to archaeologists as the Principal Bird Deity or the Celestial Bird is pictured here in an artist's preliminary rendering that reproduces the plaster veneer and cream-colored paint that originally covered the mask's stone superstructure. Built into the base of a pyramid at Nakbé in about 300 BC, the mask was deliberately hidden by later generations of Maya, who surrounded it with obscuring terraces.

root crops, vines, and beans, as well as fruits and nuts, were grown. Another technique for improving harvests and extending the quantity of arable land was the building of raised fields, a labor-intensive but high-yield approach still practiced throughout Central America.

In the late 1960s, the Canadian geographer Alfred Siemens found indelible evidence that the ancient Maya had indeed employed raised-field agriculture. Studying aerial photographs of the Candelaria River basin in the southwestern section of Yucatan, Siemens observed a distinctive mosaic of humps covering an area of swampy riverside terrain. Investigations on the ground confirmed that the Maya had reclaimed both swamps and flood plains for planting by digging drainage channels in the waterlogged soil and heaping the nutrient-rich excavated soil in mounds several feet above water level. The channels themselves provided access by boat to the fields, as well as continuing supplies of organic muck to keep the fields fertilized; readily available fish and shellfish were an additional benefit. But the question remained as to how widespread the practice had been. An answer was suggested some 10 years later by a high-technology instrument called synthetic-aperture radar, which can peer through dense vegetation and map whatever lies beneath in considerable detail. Between 1977 and 1982, airborne radar surveyed the forests of southern Mexico and Guatemala and revealed what appeared to be a vast expanse of fields and ditches in a boggy region formerly regarded as wasteland. Some of these features turned out to be natural rather than man-made, but by 1991 further studies documented scattered, if not quite so intensive, use of raised fields.

Other aerial surveys have shown that, in areas where the main problem was a shortage of water, the Maya constructed large-scale irrigation systems. At Edzná, a major city on the dry coastal plain of southwest Yucatan, a team of archaeologists led by Ray Matheny of Brigham Young University charted an elaborate canal and reservoir system constructed between 200 BC and AD 100. Among the most impressive features was a canal up to 100 yards wide and more than seven miles long running south from the city to the river. North of the city center, seven shorter canals fanned out to supply several reservoirs, the largest of which could hold 32 million gallons of water. Altogether, Matheny calculated, the people of Edzná had invested 1.68 million man-days of labor—all of it done by hand with the aid of adzes and hoes made of chert—to create a water-storage capacity of nearly 600 million gallons.

On the eastern coast of Yucatan, at the city of Cerros, the inhabitants had also built extensive waterworks. The ceremonial heart of this farming, seafaring, and trading center near the mouths of the Hondo and New rivers was separated from the mainland by a canal almost a mile long, with a feeder channel that drained a number of fields. To some archaeologists seeking clues to the evolution of Maya society, however, the chief fascination of Cerros is the apparent swiftness and purposefulness with which it embraced the institution of kingly rule.

Among those who have investigated Cerros's metamorphosis from hamlet to kingdom are two American Mayanists: Linda Schele of the University of Texas at Austin, a professional painter and art teacher turned epigrapher and one of the foremost experts in deciphering Maya glyphs; and David Freidel of Southern Methodist University in Dallas, a self-confessed "dirt" archaeologist. They have interpreted the dramatic transformation wrought at Cerros as the result of a conscious decision by specific leaders, whose names have

STONE MORE PRECIOUS THAN GOLD

Revered by the Maya for its beauty, its rarity, and its presumed powers, jade presented a serious practical challenge to ancient stone carvers. Jadeite, the form of jade found in Central America, is an exceptionally hard and dense material. To fashion it into ornaments and burial goods with the primitive tools available took ingenuity and persistence.

Flint or obsidian would have been useless against jade's hard surface. Instead, the Maya apparently used disposable implements in conjunction with abrasive powders. Large pieces of jade were halved, quartered, or sawed into flat slabs with a cord drawn repeatedly back and forth over wet sand to etch a deep groove. Wooden saws and bone drills were similarly employed to incise lines, whorls, and other designs. Sometimes jade dust was used as the abrasive material. Pieces were polished with the fibers of cane or gourds, plants that have microscopic silica deposits in their cells.

A striking number of jade human and animal figures were carved in the wedge shape of the celt—a type of chisel or ax head. Scholars speculate that Maya carvers may have routinely cut jade into that utilitarian shape with an eye toward using some as tools.

With relatively minimal additional work, those pieces with the finest color and texture were then turned into amulets and effigies, like the four-inch figure of a deity below.

Not all of the green stones the Maya carved were true jade. Modern spectrometer and chemical analysis has revealed that many artifacts once thought to be jade are in fact other minerals such as serpentine, quartz, or green albitite—materials that modern archaeologists call social jade.

Maya artisans recognized the differences, reserving the best-quality jade for objects belonging to the highest-ranking individuals and for the most important religious offerings. The impressive Preclassic jade necklace above would have proclaimed its wearer a person of power and status.

been lost but whose architectural legacy testifies to their bold initiative. The scenario Schele and Freidel have suggested, though admittedly speculative and by no means universally accepted, rings true in its depiction of the importance of individuals in the unfolding destiny of the Maya.

By about 50 BC, Cerros was already a bustling port and, because of its two rivers, served as an important connection between the Caribbean coastal trade and communities in the interior. Transport was by dugout canoe, hewn from the trunks of mahogany and other hardwoods; seagoing versions were probably more than 40 feet long and could hold as many as 50 people. Cargo headed inland would have included a broad range of local goods: fish, shellfish, and sea mammals for food; shells, sharks' teeth, and stingray spines for use in religious rituals; and salt, which was used by the Maya not only to season and preserve food but also as a form of currency and as an ingredient in medicines.

Among the most valued items to pass through Cerros would have been obsidian and jade, mined as far away as central Mexico and in a few rare places in the southern Guatemalan highlands. Obsidian, a black volcanic glass, could be chipped to a knife-edge sharpness and was thus prized for making weapons and cutting implements. Jade, of course, had great religious and ceremonial significance, and was in high demand throughout Maya territory. In exchange for these and other precious imports, lowland communities could have offered such essentials as foodstuffs, cotton, and such items as quetzal feathers and jaguar skins.

Trade would have familiarized the inhabitants of Cerros with other people's customs—including the concept of divine kingship, which had apparently already taken hold at such places as Nakbé and El Mirador. Schele and Freidel speculate that the patriarchs of Cerros realized that their city too needed the prestige of being ruled by a king—to enhance its status with trading partners—and quite deliberately picked one of their number to fill the role.

Because there are no glyphic texts at Cerros to tell the story, there is no way of knowing the precise circumstances that might have motivated the conversion of Cerros into a royal center—a process that took no more than 50 years. But the archaeological record does suggest how the transformation was achieved. After destroying their old homes, the people scattered jade jewelry and the broken vessels of a ritual feast over the ruins, where the new ceremonial structures would rise. New dwellings were built in an arc around the cleared area. Custom dictated that a house's door should face the rising sun, but some members of the community positioned their doorways facing the emergent symbol of royal power—the temple being constructed at the water's edge.

Similar in plan to the ceremonial pyramids at Nakbé, this first temple at Cerros bore facades adorned with divine images that Schele and Freidel believe were intended to legitimize the kings of Cerros as descendants of the gods. Although these pictorial messages can be ambiguous, Schele found that they contained strategically placed individual glyphs that helped clarify their meaning. Thus a four-petaled glyph—a symbol known to stand for the sun—appearing on a snarling animal mask identified it as the Jaguar Sun God, a deity representing not only the sun but also the younger of the Hero Twins, the prototypes of Maya kingship.

As Schele and Freidel surmised from their study of inscriptions elsewhere, the temple had functioned as a public stage for one of the most sacred Maya rites—the king's communing with the gods and ancestors, known as a journey to the Underworld. To achieve the rapturous, hallucinatory state that made this spiritual journey possible, the king would fast and engage in bloodletting. The layout of the temple interior suggested that the king performed this last task in private, in a small room at the eastern corner of the temple, and that he then returned to public view at the top of the temple's stairway ready to begin the divine communion, his white cotton garments stained with blood.

Although such practices as bloodletting seem barbaric to modern sensibilities, to the Maya their importance was quite literally earth-shattering. They believed that the universe was filled with dangerous and explosive forces that could only be contained by the

Built around 50 BC at the edge of Chetumal Bay on the eastern coast of Yucatan, the first temple at Cerros faced inland toward an urban center covering 160 acres. A few years later, the people who occupied this thriving hub of Maya trade built an even larger temple complex or acropolis on a raised plaza accessible by a grand stairway that rose up the front of the pyramid.

proper rituals. Stars and planets were regarded as the visible manifestations of gods, and because their movements in the heavens could be either beneficial or harmful, Maya nobility tracked these movements with exquisite care *(pages 130-133)*. The darkening of the sun in an eclipse, for instance, was perceived as a form of death, one from which the sun might not recover. The first seasonal appearance of the evening star, actually the planet Venus, was taken as a signal of coming war. By timing public rituals such as bloodletting to coincide with calendrical and celestial cycles, Maya rulers attempted to control these events, confirming that the king was vital to the maintenance of cosmic order.

Not many years after the building of this temple at Cerros, work began nearby on a much larger structure that consisted of three different platform levels. Occupying an area three times that of the original temple, the complex stood more than 50 feet high, which meant that rituals conducted at its summit would have been invisible to people on the ground. On this topmost plaza, according to Schele and Freidel, the king performed his bloodletting rites in full view of a privileged few. Attended by this elite, the king then descended the

The snarling features of the Jaguar Sun God are still discernible in the stonework on the lower platform of Cerros's first temple; the huge visage above it is thought to represent the morning star. The two masks were part of a quartet flanking the temple stairs and symbolizing the physical passage of the sun.

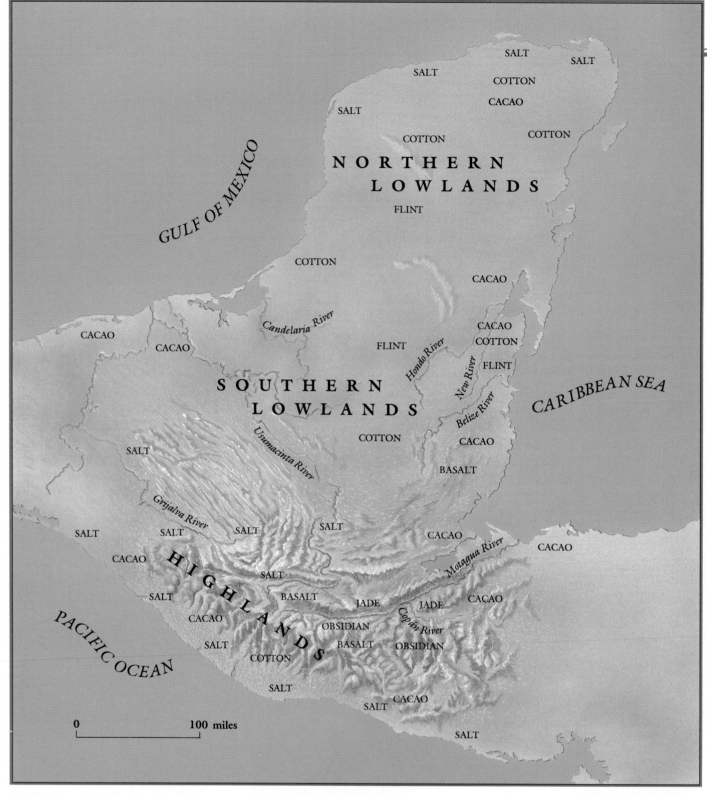

SALT
SALT   SALT
COTTON
CACAO
SALT
COTTON   COTTON

**NORTHERN
LOWLANDS**

FLINT

COTTON
CACAO

CACAO
COTTON
FLINT

Candelaria River

CACAO   CACAO   FLINT   CACAO   FLINT

**SOUTHERN
LOWLANDS**

Hondo River   *New River*

Usumacinta River   *Belize River*

COTTON   CACAO

SALT   BASALT

Grijalva River   SALT   SALT

CACAO   CACAO

SALT   SALT   SALT   *Motagua River*

SALT   CACAO

HIGHLANDS

CACAO   SALT   BASALT   JADE   JADE   CACAO

SALT   CACAO   OBSIDIAN   *Copán River*

SALT   COTTON   BASALT   OBSIDIAN

SALT

SALT   CACAO

SALT

GULF OF MEXICO

CARIBBEAN SEA

PACIFIC OCEAN

0   100 miles

Major items of trade and their places of origin are shown on this map of Maya territory. From the earliest times, Maya villagers living in coastal communities exchanged salt, fish, and other marine resources for the agricultural produce of their inland neighbors, often using navigable rivers to transport goods. As the culture evolved, so did a taste for luxury goods from distant places. Among these were feathers, shells, jaguar skins, tobacco, jade, and obsidian. By the time of Columbus's fourth voyage to the Americas in 1502, merchants were plying the seas from Mexico to Panama in enormous canoes, their hulls filled with great quantities of valuable raw materials and manufactured items for trade.

64

stairs to a larger, intermediate platform. Though not as exclusive as the upper platform, this viewing area was nevertheless reserved for a high-ranking minority of members of the royal court, who, swelling the king's entourage, followed him down into the immense lower plaza where the common people waited.

By the time this second temple-pyramid was completed, the first king of Cerros apparently had died; his jade royal insignia—pieces of a headband and an ornament worn on the chest—were found buried just below the summit of the second temple. Perhaps not content with the existing complex, the new ruler built two more temples. One, facing the rising sun, was intended as a royal tomb. The other, facing west, seems to have commemorated ritual warfare, when kings and nobles would go into battle not to kill but to capture enemy royalty and bring them back to be tortured and sacrificed; this temple's facade was adorned with carvings of human heads and images of jaguar heads with scrolls (thought to represent blood) issuing from their mouths—all symbols of royal power, which would have been demonstrated to the people by the decapitation of high-born prisoners of war.

Such a fate may have befallen the king who built the east- and west-facing temples at Cerros: He presumably died away from home, for he never occupied his tomb, which was left open. His successor began the construction of yet another temple, but the workmanship was poor, and the structure was never completed. Some change that affected regal authority had taken place, though what it was is pure guesswork. Perhaps the king's power had been broken by an external enemy, or it may have been crippled by internal revolt. In any event, despite his semidivine status, a Maya ruler was judged by his performance, and if a successor turned out to be weak, incompetent, or simply unlucky, he would not have lasted. The failure to complete the new temple certainly proved the point at Cerros, marking the end of the royal line. Shortly after-

Highly prized spondylus *shells, jade, and obsidian, imported over long distances, were found cached at the Preclassic site of Cuello, located near the New River in Belize. Maya merchants may have exchanged cotton, raw (as below) or woven into cloth, for the ancient valuables.*

Caribbean stingray spines like this one, found at Cuello, were among the implements Maya rulers used to lacerate themselves in their efforts to communicate with the gods.

In a bloodletting ritual depicted on a lintel from Yaxchilan, ruler Shield-Jaguar holds a torch over his wife, Lady Xoc, as she pulls a thorn-barbed rope through her tongue.

Lady Xoc gazes up at the apparition of a warrior emerging from the mouth of a Vision Serpent. The serpent rises from a shallow bowl containing lancets and pieces of bark paper soaked with Lady Xoc's blood, suggesting that the vision materialized from it. Participants in such rituals may have hallucinated because of massive blood loss.

ward, the populace ritually destroyed the symbols of regal power by setting great fires against the facades of the temples and smashing parts of the masks. The experiment with kingship was over.

Like Cerros, the great metropolis of El Mirador suffered a terminal decline in the first century AD, possibly because its trading relationships had broken down. Only 40 miles to the south, two other Maya cities, Tikal and Uaxactún, were well placed to succeed as the area's economic and political powers. Blessed with fertile soils and abundant supplies of chert, these communities bridged a portage between two major river systems—one flowing northeast to the Caribbean, the other west to the Gulf of Mexico. Less than a day's walk separated the two cities, so they were bound to come into competition. Perhaps because it had a somewhat more advantageous location, Tikal seems to have risen to preeminence, possibly establishing better relations with Teotihuacan, the magnificent city and mercantile center that dominated the Valley of Mexico during the third and fourth centuries AD. The rivalry between Tikal and Uaxactún eventually grew violent and was ultimately settled through warfare toward the end of the fourth century AD. To the victor went the prize of its defeated neighbor's kingdom and, more significantly, control of a vital sector of the entire central-lowland trade network.

The ruins of Tikal's largest temple-pyramid still soar above 200-foot-tall mahogany, cedar, and chicle trees in the midst of one of Central America's densest jungles. Although Cortés and his army must have passed nearby on their way to Honduras in 1525, the city was not officially rediscovered until 1848. For more than a century, the only means of access were rough trails hacked by collectors of raw chewing gum, so most early expeditions remained small-scale. The Guatemalan air force eventually built a small dirt runway beside the ruins in 1951, and five years later the University of Pennsylvania mounted an unprecedented research program at the site. The project lasted 15 years, employing a total of more than 100 archaeologists and proving to be one of the most extensive investigations ever undertaken in the New World.

With 500 buildings excavated, William Coe, director of the project during its final seven years, was able to produce a detailed reconstruction of the city's architectural history. From its modest beginnings as a farming village sometime before 600 BC, Tikal developed into a substantial community during the next few centuries.

MESSAGES FROM THE CLAY

At first glance, the two polychrome pots seen here look different enough to have been created by separate masters. But scientific detective work has shown otherwise. What is more, the methods used to determine their authorship and place of origin will help scholars identify other pots for which there is no provenance, an especially acute problem in Maya studies, where too often objects turn out to have been dug illegally and sold without background information accompanying them.

Glyphs on these pots include the painter's name and show that he was related to nobility, Ruler 3 of Naranjo and Lady Shell-Star of Yaxha, and suggest that the artist may have been a second son of the royal household. The glyphs below give the still-to-be-deciphered name.

The archaeologist Michael Coe of Yale University was not only convinced that these two pots were by one artist, despite their seeming disparities, but also that they came from Naranjo, in Guatemala, about 25 miles east of Tikal. Intensive study of the vases by the art historian Dorie Reents-Budet of the Duke University Museum would confirm this.

Thanks to strides made in the decipherment of glyphs, translation of the stylistically similar writing on the sides of the pots identified both the artist's name and that of the patron or owner of each vessel. But if further proof of a single creator were needed, it came when a chemical test was carried out on minute samples from each vase. The profile of the trace elements they contained showed they had been formed from the same mixture of clay and other ingredients. Moreover, their chemical profile matched that of potsherds found at Naranjo, thus establishing the location of the royal workshop where they were created.

As early as the second century BC, great plazas had taken shape, and these became the focus of an urban core that, together with densely populated outlying settlements covering 25 square miles, housed some 40,000 inhabitants at Tikal's zenith.

In the first century BC, a complex of monumental structures and royal burial vaults was built in the central area. Known as the North Acropolis, it was a resting place not only for the bones and regalia of kings but also for the remains of an emerging class of hereditary elite. Analysis has revealed that the individuals interred here were taller and more robust than the common people, a sign that they had enjoyed a better diet and, perhaps, that their rank owed at least in part to an inherited physical superiority.

The occupant of one of the richest tombs was a woman, indicating that high status was now the birthright of both the men and the women of elite families. This same tomb was adorned with images of nobles, possibly her kinsmen or ancestors. An early example of Maya portraiture, these depictions represent the shift away from the dedication of ritual art exclusively to the gods. More paintings, tentatively identified by Schele and Freidel as portraits of the king himself and his nobles, decorated the outside of a nearby shrine whose interior had been blackened by sacrificial fires.

At Uaxactún, to the north, archaeologists have discovered further dramatic evidence of a move toward the personal—the first known instances of Maya kings memorializing themselves in sculpture. As at Tikal, large-scale expansion and remodeling of the city's ceremonial hub occurred between the first and third centuries AD. Trench excavations in 1985 came upon an extraordinary group of six temples from this period that had been buried under later buildings erected on a small acropolis. Their facades were covered with the most extensive array of Preclassic stucco masks yet found. The largest individual mask is an ambitious depiction of the Maya cosmos, showing on one level a great monster in the primordial sea, and on the level above an identical monster representing the sacred mountain that rose from the waters to form dry land. The head of this monster is penetrated by the so-called Vision Serpent—a snake that symbolized the path to the Underworld taken by the king when he communicated with the ancestral dead and the gods in bloodletting rites.

The mythological imagery was intriguing in its details and its symbolism, but what was truly different on one building were the sculpted portraits of a ruler, wearing the recognizable costume of a king and standing on a *pop,* or throne mat. Perhaps most significant of all, the sculptures were placed on the front surface of a temple that served as a gateway and processional entrance to the acropolis. In years to come, kings throughout the Maya region would erect the steles that record their reigns in words and pictures in similarly prominent positions.

Establishing kingship was one thing, but as the inhabitants of Cerros must have known, making it last was quite another. At Tikal the foundations of an enduring dynasty were laid by a king who ruled early in the third century AD and whose importance as an ancestral figure was acknowledged in inscriptions commissioned by some of his 39 successors, who continued to hold the throne for an astonishing 600 years. The first of these to be portrayed in a carving was a character who has been dubbed by epigraphers Scroll-Ahau-Jaguar—like other Maya rulers' names, a shorthand description of the glyphs identifying him. ("Ahau" is the Maya word for "lord.") His figure appears on perhaps the most famous stele ever discovered—the one bearing a Maya date corresponding to July 8, AD 292, the oldest example of Maya dating on a monument, and the traditional marker of the commencement of the Classic period.

Three decades later, Tikal's monarch was a man known as Moon-Zero-Bird, who is represented on a royal belt ornament standing on top of a prostrate captive of evident nobility. This was a typical representation of the standard form of Maya warfare, the hand-to-hand combat whose chief aim was the demonstration of personal prowess through the taking of prisoners. From the beginning of the fourth century, images of bound captives recur at both Tikal and Uaxactún, suggesting that their respective rulers regarded their neighbors as a source of sacrificial victims to commemorate accessions and other ritual events. The relationship between the two cities could hardly have been peaceful even if the rules of engagement were preventing out-and-out conflict.

Soon enough, however, the rivalry did come to a head, during the reign of Great-Jaguar-Paw, the ninth ruler of Tikal's long-lasting dynasty, who acceded sometime around the middle of the fourth century. The first Maya expert to suggest the possibility that the nature of the cities' war making had changed was Peter Mathews of the University of Calgary. In the course of studying steles, he realized that there was one at each site that recorded the same date and the same action by a nobleman; Mathews figured that the event had been

Found in the tomb of a Tikal ruler, a terra-cotta censer in the form of the god believed to be the deity of human sacrifice by decapitation leers at a severed head balanced on the plate in his hands. When Tikal vanquished neighboring Uaxactún, the captives were probably beheaded in honor of this macabre deity.

either an alliance by marriage or a conquest. When Schele and Freidel examined the evidence, they concluded that the steles were war monuments celebrating the capture of Uaxactún on January 16, 378, by a Tikal lord called Smoking-Frog.

The Tikal stele was erected 50 years after the event it commemorates and reports that Great-Jaguar-Paw sanctified the victory by an act of bloodletting. Other inscriptions have established that Smoking-Frog was Great-Jaguar-Paw's brother and, most likely, his war chief. He appears on the stele at Uaxactún wearing a large spherical headdress, bearing in one hand an obsidian-studded club and in the other a spear-thrower, also known as an atlatl—a device used to propel a javelin with great force.

Smoking-Frog's accouterments, particularly his headdress and spear-thrower, were a radical departure from the costume and weaponry of earlier Maya lords. Linda Schele and David Freidel, among others, have come to believe that they were adopted from Teotihuacan as part of a new military cult, which John Carlson has proposed was centered on the supposed influence of the motions of the planet Venus. Teotihuacan, which apparently dominated central Mexico through warfare with lesser neighbors, had probably been trading with the two Maya cities since at least the first century AD. An elaborately decorated pottery vase found at Tikal and dating to the time of Tikal's triumph provides confirmation of good relations: It shows six emissaries from Teotihuacan, identifiable by their garb, being greeted by a Maya representative. It is not unreasonable to imagine that contact with Teotihuacan might have provided the motive for the war between Tikal and Uaxactún, encouraging each side to fight for control of the trade route through its territory.

No account of the actual battle has survived, but the likelihood is that with the stakes so high, the old rules fell by the wayside. This, after all, was a war of conquest, presumably fought without quarter by warriors armed with spear-throwers, which could launch a deadly rain of projectiles on the enemy from a distance. And when Smoking-Frog triumphed, he was not content merely to take the king of Uaxactún captive; he occupied the city itself, making himself its master. Within a year of his victory, Smoking-Frog succeeded his brother, but he chose to rule from his new possession. Archaeologists have noted that from this time, architectural features once associated exclusively with Tikal begin to appear at Uaxactún.

Those losers not killed in battle suffered the traditional fate. In a temple near the stele at Uaxactún recording Smoking-Frog's achievement, archaeologists found five skeletons of women and infants who may very well have been the vanquished king's wives and children, slaughtered to bring his dynasty to an end. At Tikal, an inscription commemorating the victory uses a glyph in the shape of a god of human sacrifice, shown elsewhere seated on a stool of bones holding a severed human head on a plate.

Tikal was the predominant, most prestigious city of the central lowlands for nearly 200 years. It presumably went about extending its influence, establishing connections with Maya cities possibly as far away as Copán, situated on the southeastern edge of Maya territory. Throughout the region, new dynasties came to power at various cities, but it was likely that they all regarded Tikal with special reverence; its royal line, perhaps the oldest of the lot, symbolized the importance of connections with the past, with the world of ancestors and supernatural power that invigorated every kind of political and social endeavor. Indeed, the entire Maya civilization seemed well nourished, already blossoming, and heading into its most glorious, full-flowering days.

PARTING THE MISTS OF TIME

Fully a millennium after Tikal's decline, the soaring spires of the city's temple-pyramids still rise above the Guatemalan jungle. Not even the fog banks rolling in from the nearby Caribbean can obscure the loftiest of these shrines *(above)*, the thousand-year-old Temple of the Jaguar Priests (also known as Temple III), which soars to a height of 180 feet.

Dating to the golden age of the Maya, such structures proclaim a civilization magnificent in its complexity and extent. Archaeological excavations conducted over the course of more than three decades have only succeeded in plucking six square miles of the metropolis's approximately 25-square-mile sprawl from the jungle's tenacious grasp. Yet within this small precinct alone—the very heart of Tikal—lie more than 3,000 buildings and more than 200 stone monuments.

That such archaeological riches have been revealed in so small an area is a testament not only to Tikal's astounding vitality but to its amazing longevity as well.

From obscure Preclassic beginnings in the Petén rain forest of northern Guatemala 2,600 years ago, Tikal rose to become the premier trading center of the central lowlands and the flower of eighth-century Classic Maya culture. Imposing steles, or commemorative stones covered with hieroglyphs, labyrinthine palaces, and colossal temples proclaimed the city's might, and carvings and sculptures depicting deities, fantastically ornamented rulers, and vanquished foes expressed the power base of this supremely class-conscious society—one increasingly steeped in blood.

In its heyday, all the prodigious energies and talents of Tikal's inhabitants—from rulers to peasants—were directed toward sustaining and expanding the city's glory. Like the illustrious structures of Rome and ancient Egypt's pharaonic Thebes, the buildings of Tikal became more than emblems of a proud and powerful civilization. For the Maya, they were the repositories of power itself.

Revealing 10 centuries of neglect, the excavated ruins of Tikal still gleam in their rain-forest surroundings. The green expanse at center marks the Great Plaza with its stately complement of Temples I (left) and II (right); in the foreground lies the North Acropolis with its ancestral shrines. The imposing palaces of the Central Acropolis loom to the rear.

Great builder and ruler Ah Cacaw, credited with ushering in Tikal's golden age, appears in symbolic military regalia on this stele erected in AD 711. Staring to his right beneath an elaborate feather headdress, the ruler clutches a ritual staff. A divination bag dangles from his right wrist. Ah Cacaw commissioned the memorial in the 29th year of his reign.

The ceremonial heart of Tikal is restored to its ninth-century splendor in this rendering by Canadian architect Stanley Loten. While people scurry between the ornamented temples of the North Acropolis (foreground) and the Great Plaza (center), and bureaucrats and royalty mill about the halls of the Central Acropolis (rear), the seated image of Ah Cacaw looks down from the top of Temple I.

A GRAND AND GLORIOUS CITY

In 1961, archaeologists tunneling below Tikal's Temple I happened upon a vaulted chamber containing a skeleton splendidly adorned with jade, pearls, and shells, and surrounded by other treasures. This was the tomb of Ah Cacaw, the greatest of the city's sovereigns. With his accession in AD 682, Tikal embarked on an age of expansion that, over the next 100 years, revived its domination of the region.

During his five-decade reign, Ah Cacaw shifted the city's ritual hub from the old North Acropolis to the Great Plaza, where he commissioned the construction of Temples I and II. Their lavish ornamentation and imposing height—roughly 140 feet—eclipsed all previous structures, setting the standard for subsequent Maya architecture.

Under Ah Cacaw's son, Ruler B (also called Yaxkin) and grandson, Chitam, Tikal blossomed into a major city—with perhaps 40,000 inhabitants at its peak—complete with gigantic temple-pyramids, palace compound, ball courts, marketplace, and sweathouse.

ROOMS FIT FOR A KING

While archaeological evidence indicates that Tikal's peasantry once dwelled in far-flung cottage communities, royalty inhabited the more circumscribed neighborhood of the Central Acropolis—which, by Late Classic times, had become a four-acre maze of buildings surrounding six spacious courts.

Despite the amenities of the palaces, life in the compound had its drawbacks. Tikal's architects—pressured by a burgeoning nobility—were kept busy continually dividing and redividing rooms, walling up doorways, and adding stairways and stories. By the halcyon days of the redoubtable Ah Cacaw, the acropolis had become a labyrinth of halls and passageways, cool by day, warm by night.

The buildings themselves were rarely more than two galleries wide, with all the rooms close to exits. In addition to sheltering the elite, they probably served as administrative centers. Evidence exists to support the assumption that the porches of the buildings had awnings, which would have made it possible to carry on daytime activities outdoors, protected from the elements.

Traces of the frieze that once encircled the outside of Teobert Maler's palace are barely discernible above its doorways, once shaded by colorful cotton awnings. Inside, the palace is remarkably well preserved. Maler, an early researcher at Tikal, lived here in relative comfort during his explorations in 1895 and 1904.

This room of the so-called Five-Story Palace—with its original stone bench and beams of worm-resistant chicozapote wood surviving—probably housed some of the elite. The narrowness of the chamber was dictated by its overarching corbel vault, which transferred the weight of the ceiling to the walls. Such vaults were a classic feature of Maya stone architecture.

The top three stories of the Five-Story Palace (above, right) preside over the intimate confines of Court 4 in a reconstruction of the southern Central Acropolis as it was during Ah Cacaw's reign.

THE PROVINCE OF GOD-KINGS

Nothing so evinced the brilliance of Tikal as its grand temples. Masterfully engineered to inspire awe, these towering shrines comprised three parts: a pyramidal base spanned by a stairway, a chambered sanctuary, and a "roof comb"—a sweep of strictly ornamental masonry that stretched heavenward from the sanctuary's own roof.

It is unlikely that the common people ever ascended the stairs. Watched by a spellbound populace, kings and their assistants in rituals would mount the steps and disappear into the sanctuary, where they probably performed religious ceremonies. Later on they emerged, attired in gorgeous raiment, to conduct public rites of worship and perhaps offer up human sacrifice.

Such sublime drama was doubtless played out regularly in Temples I through V, built during Tikal's Late Classic period. Stuccoed a brilliant white, their sculptures painted in dazzling hues of red, green, blue, and yellow, they were the focal point of the city's ceremonial life until AD 900, when Chichén Itzá superseded Tikal and the temples were abandoned to the ages.

Nine terraces (9 is a sacred Maya number) rise to the base of the roof comb of Temple I, photographed at sunset.

The Maya incorporated vaulted hollows inside roof combs, as can be seen in this cross section of Temple I, to reduce their weight. Within the temple's underlying sanctuary, three corbeled chambers—one set behind the other—served as reliquaries, chapels, or ceremonial staging areas.

Temple III's prodigious roof comb, its stuccoed finish eroded away, bestrides the Petén jungle. Temple III is thought to have been built by Ah Cacaw's grandson.

ROYALTY AND THE SEEDS OF DOOM

Deep within the crumbling pyramid supporting the mysterious Temple of Inscriptions at Palenque, the noted Mexican archaeologist Alberto Ruz was about to make one of the most significant discoveries in the entire history of Maya archaeology. He and a team of workmen, who had been digging at the site for four long seasons, were clearing rubble from the end of a corridor when, according to Ruz, "the foreman, half frightened, felt his crowbar sink into emptiness." Ruz instructed him to remove more debris, and a narrow gap appeared. Shining a floodlight through the opening, Ruz peered inside. Thick deposits of lime clung to the walls like a glittering web of glass, giving the darkened chamber a markedly surreal appearance.

"Out of the dim shadows emerged a vision from a fairy tale," Ruz later wrote, "a fantastic, ethereal sight from another world. It seemed a huge magic grotto carved out of ice, the walls sparkling and glistening like snow crystals. Delicate festoons of stalactites hung like tassels of a curtain, and the stalagmites on the floor looked like drippings from a great candle. The impression, in fact, was that of an abandoned chapel. Across the walls marched stucco figures in low relief. Then my eyes sought the floor. This was almost entirely filled with a great carved stone slab, in perfect condition. As I gazed in awe and astonishment, I described the marvelous sight to my colleagues

Powerful ruler 18-Rabbit gazes regally at the viewer in this stele found in the civic and ceremonial center at Copán. During his reign, art in the great city reached a pinnacle of sophistication.

. . . but they wouldn't believe me until they had pushed me aside and had seen with their own eyes the fascinating spectacle. Ours were the first eyes that had gazed on it in more than a thousand years!"

When Ruz began his investigations at Palenque in 1949, he could not have guessed that the ancient site would yield such a thrilling secret. For as he would learn, this strange underground chamber contained not only an unprecedented cache of artifacts but also the sarcophagus of a Maya ruler who had been buried in the grandest of styles. It was one of the first times a tomb had been found within a Maya pyramid, and the discovery would open fresh insights into the Maya world—particularly the latter stages of that most glorious phase known as the Classic period. In the years to come, this and other similarly groundbreaking pieces of evidence would show Maya kingship in its full majesty and power, and in the process provide tantalizing clues about what had sent such a spectacular and sophisticated culture on its final downward spiral.

In its own day, Ruz's remarkable find made an astounding impression. Although scores of other distinguished archaeologists had visited the Temple of Inscriptions over the years, attracted by the intriguing hieroglyphs that gave the structure its name, none had

Behind the palace at Palenque—topped with an unusual four-story tower that perhaps served as an astronomical observatory—looms the Temple of Inscriptions. The most impressive pyramid tomb on the American continent, the temple housed the remains of seventh-century Maya ruler Pacal. In its heyday, the ancient city dazzled the eye with buildings of red stucco, their decorations painted in vivid yellows, blues, and greens.

suspected that a burial chamber lay hidden deep within the pyramid. Even Ruz, just appointed director of research at Palenque by Mexico's National Institute of Anthropology and History, was slow to realize what an extraordinary trail he was on. Indeed, as he launched his first season of digging, the excavation seemed as if it were going to be quite routine.

As work progressed, however, Ruz found his attention repeatedly drawn to a curious detail of the temple's interior. Unlike most Maya sanctuaries, whose floors were covered with a finishing layer of stucco, the main chamber of the Temple of Inscriptions had a foundation of exposed flagstone. And in the very center was an especially large stone that had two rows of holes drilled through it, each one filled with a stone plug. For some time scholars had been pondering what this odd feature signified, but as yet no one had advanced a plausible explanation.

The drilled flagstone intrigued Ruz. Again and again he found himself examining the floor in search of a solution to the puzzle. Then, one day, as he studied the point at which the walls of the interior chamber met the flagstone floor, he felt a sudden shock of recognition. It was then, he later wrote, likening his investigation to that of a private detective, "that I found the cigarette butt of the criminal—the architectural detail that gave a certain clue: The walls of the temple continued beneath the floor, proving that originally some construction on a lower level was connected with the temple."

Plunging through the floor of the Temple of Inscriptions and into its pyramid foundation, this glistening vaulted stairway (top)—once filled with 600,000 pounds of rubble—descends 73 feet to the burial chamber housing Pacal's magnificent limestone tomb (above). The crypt measures 12 feet across at its widest point.

As for the drilled flagstone, in all likelihood ancient workmen had passed ropes through the holes and used them to lower this final block of flooring into place. By plugging up the holes, they apparently had intended to seal whatever lay beneath—some kind of chamber, perhaps—for all time.

No sooner had he reached this startling conclusion than Ruz resolved to test his theory by digging into the floor, choosing to work just adjacent to the drilled slab where some of the flagstones had already been broken up or removed, presumably by earlier treasure seekers. At first it appeared that his excitement had been unfounded: All that Ruz and his colleagues discovered was a narrow opening choked with limestone and debris. As they began to clear the rubble away, however, the first of a series of stone steps appeared, apparently leading down into the pyramid. But to penetrate farther, they would have to remove the large stones and clay that blocked their way. The heat, humidity, and choking dust created stifling working conditions, and the rocks became increasingly awkward to remove. "So difficult was the work," Ruz recalled, "the breaking up of the rubble packing and the lifting out of the stones with ropes and pulleys, that in the first season's labor, we got only 23 steps down—about eight steps a month."

After four seasons of backbreaking labor, Ruz's team had managed to clear the vaulted stairway to a depth of 73 feet. Two seemingly minor discoveries relieved the tedium of their efforts.

Mythological scenes carved in relief on the 10,000-pound limestone slab covering Pacal's coffin depict the ruler at the moment of his death. In the center, Pacal tumbles into the Underworld, dragged downward by the tentacle-like snouts of dragons, while the axis mundi, *or World Tree, rises behind him, crowned by a heavenly bird. Rimming the lid are images that illustrate the sun's daily westward progression into night.*

First, Ruz unearthed a small masonry box containing two earrings carved in jade, that most precious material the Maya so often associated with royalty. Second, the digging on the stairway exposed the opening of a strange hollow duct. The small shaft, which was set directly into the lime mortar of the passage wall, appeared to wind downward into the core of the pyramid. Ruz could not even guess at its function.

At last, toward the close of the summer season of 1952, the countless hours of excavation seemed about to bear fruit. Ruz and his crew reached the bottom of the stairway and broke through a tightly packed wall of rubble into a sealed antechamber. The small, cramped room, which was blocked at the far end by another wall, held a cache of ceremonial objects—seven beads and two earplugs made of jade, three ceramic dishes, two shells filled with cinnabar, and a large tear-shaped pearl. Ruz knew at once that the items represented some sort of ritual offering to the gods. He also realized that something of great importance must lie beyond the sealed-off opening at the opposite end of the chamber. Once more, the crew set to digging.

Penetrating this barrier proved to be the most difficult labor of the entire expedition. Water seeping down through the pyramid had mixed with the limestone mortar, turning the whole wall, which was 12 feet thick, rock hard. "For a full week we toiled to break it down," Ruz recounted, "at times even having to break the solid stones, so firmly had the mass solidified. The men were almost buried in the damp lime, which burned and cracked their hands, to a point almost beyond endurance."

Eventually the workers broke through, only to come upon still another antechamber. At its far end, at the foot of another blocking wall, they found a crude masonry chest taking up 12 square feet. Nothing in Ruz's archaeological experience had prepared him for the grisly sight that greeted him as he raised the lid. Inside the chest, covered with a layer of stone and debris, were six human skeletons. Although the remains were poorly preserved, it was clear that at least one of the interred was a female, and all had apparently died at 17 or 18 years of age. For Ruz, only one conclusion was pos-

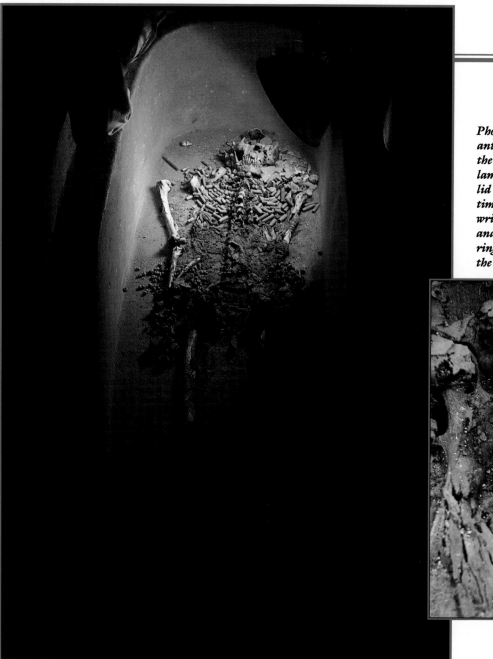

Photographed in late 1952 by Mexican anthropologist Arturo Romano Pacheco, the bones of Lord Pacal are revealed by lamplight after the massive sarcophagus lid is raised from the coffin for the first time in 1,300 years (left). Each of Pacal's wrists bore a bracelet of 200 jade beads, and his left hand, adorned with jade rings, clutched a ball also sculpted from the precious stone (below).

sible. "Unquestionably," he declared, "this was a human sacrifice."

As he reflected on his find, Ruz's mind raced ahead to an even more dramatic possibility. He surmised that the spirits of the skeletons heaped at his feet were probably intended to stand guard forever over the body of a departed Maya ruler. Chances were that body lay close at hand. With a sense of mounting anticipation, Ruz and his team pressed forward. Beyond the masonry crypt of the sacrificial victims stood a wall of rubble, the one that his foreman soon accidentally broke through. Nearby was a low triangular doorway sealed with a single enormous stone, and although Ruz had been able to peek into the chamber beyond, two more days of digging would pass

Reassembled from some 200 jade fragments resting upon and beside Pacal's skull, this life-size jade mask with mother-of-pearl and obsidian eyes covered the ruler's face—which had been stripped of its skin—after his death. Set in the mouth of the mask is a T-shaped amulet, sign of Pacal's elevation to godhood.

before the triangular stone could be moved enough to permit entry. At last, on July 15, 1952, Ruz squeezed through the opening and descended the final five steps into the lime-encrusted room.

"I entered the mysterious chamber," said Ruz, "with the strange sensation natural for the first one to tread the entrance steps in a thousand years. I tried to see it all with the same vision that the Palenque priests had when they left the crypt; I wanted to efface the centuries and hear the vibrations of the last human voices beneath these massive vaults; I strove to capture the cryptic message that those men of old had given us so inviolate. Across the impenetrable veil of time I sought the impossible bond between their lives and ours."

As the beam of his floodlight played about the chamber, Ruz caught sight of an immense raised platform, which he had earlier mistaken for the floor. The yellowish-white slab of limestone, of the kind that the sculptors of Palenque usually employed for particularly important works, rested on a thick pedestal buttressed by six additional rectangles of stone. Measuring more than 12 feet in length and seven feet across, the surface of the platform displayed a delicately carved relief, now acknowledged as one of the most extraordinary Maya carvings ever discovered. It showed a bejeweled figure falling into the open jaws of an earth monster, a scene that has since been understood to represent the departed soul's journey to Xibalba, the realm of the Underworld gods.

After a brief examination, Ruz drilled a hole in one corner of the slab and determined that it was hollow. The archaeologist, who had first thought this massive block might be an altar, now dared to hope that what he had found was the lid to a sarcophagus. Later, using automobile jacks reinforced with logs, his workmen began to raise the five-ton slab—inch by inch. When they had lifted it high enough to glimpse underneath, they found a second limestone slab with a peculiar curved outline. "At either end was a pair of round holes, fitted with stone plugs exactly like those we had found in the temple floor above us," Ruz recalled. "By now we knew that these were lifting holes."

"We worked on, breathless with excitement," the archaeologist continued. "Every time we jacked the great carved top up an inch we slipped a section of board under it so that, if a jack slipped, the massive sculpture would not fall. When we had raised it about 15 inches, my curiosity got the best of me."

While his colleagues watched anxiously, Ruz wriggled beneath the raised slab and climbed directly onto the inner covering. Sandwiched between the two enormous blocks, he began a preliminary examination. Removing a stone plug from one end of the inner cover, Ruz peered through the tiny hole.

"My first impression," he wrote, "was that of a mosaic of green, red, and white. Then it resolved itself into details—green jade ornaments, red painted teeth and bones, and fragments of a mask." In an instant, the archaeologist knew that his four years of effort had yielded a spectacular result. "I was gazing at the death face of him for whom all this stupendous work—the crypt, the sculpture, the stairway, the great pyramid with its crowning temple—had been built."

Only now, as he found himself literally face to face with someone who had obviously been one of the most honored individuals in Palenque's entire history, did Ruz fully appreciate the breathtaking implications of his discovery. Previously, historians and scholars had no notion that Maya pyramids, like those of the Egyptians, had served as funeral crypts for their nobles and kings. Even Ruz himself initially assumed that this particular example represented a rare exception, perhaps unique in the Maya world. In time, however, additional pyramid tombs were unearthed throughout the region, and in each case it was clear that a virtual army of engineers, artists,

"Though not of great size, Piedras Negras is remarkable for the number and superb quality of its sculptured monuments," wrote Maya scholar Tatiana Proskouriakoff, who painted this reconstruction of the acropolis at the Classic Maya site in Guatemala. Its stepped pyramids, courtyards, and temples echo the civic and ceremonial centers of larger Classical-period cities, such as Copán.

stonemasons, and laborers had been pressed into service to create a lasting tribute.

Later, when he had the opportunity to study the remains at length, Ruz was struck by the unparalleled splendor of the funerary sacraments. The body was all but covered in precious jewels and adornments. An elaborate breastplate, featuring 189 pieces of finely polished jade, lay across the exposed rib cage. Rings and bracelets hung loosely from the bones of the hands and wrists, and a diadem formed of tiny jade disks crowned the skull. A cube of jade sat in the palm of the right hand, a sphere in the left hand, both presumably priceless symbols of the departed's rank. None of the fundamental Maya funeral rites had been overlooked. In keeping with a longstanding tradition that scholars knew of from other evidence, a single jade bead had been placed in the dead man's mouth to enable the spirit to purchase food in the afterlife.

Near the head of the sarcophagus, Ruz discovered an opening in the shape of a serpent's skull. It proved to be the outlet of the curious duct he had discovered set into the limestone mortar of the passageway above. The stone shaft ran along the side of the stairway, forming a crude conduit between the burial chamber and the temple. Ruz speculated that it may have been designed as some sort of speaking tube, perhaps used by Maya priests to chant incantations into the tomb. Communications may also have passed in the opposite direction, allowing the temple priests to receive direct counsel from the spirit world. The archaeologist dubbed the strange construction a psychic duct—a channel between the world of the living and the realm of the dead.

Even as the tomb surrendered one ancient secret after another, an overriding question remained: Who was this nobleman whose passing had inspired such pageantry? A possible answer would not emerge for more than 15 years and would have to await a series of advances in the decipherment of Maya glyphs. In the late 1960s, on the basis of phonetic readings of a number of inscriptions found in the temple and the tomb, David Kelley of the University of Calgary and Floyd Lounsbury of Yale University declared that his name was Pacal, "Shield," and that he had been the ruling lord of Palenque for nearly seven decades, from AD 615 to 683.

Although scholars concur that Pacal had reigned in Palenque during this time and indeed had built this memorial to himself, a definitive identification of the actual remains has proved maddeningly elusive. Ruz himself has pointed out that analysis of the bones in the sarcophagus seemed to indicate that they belonged to a man only 40 years old, whereas the true Lord Pacal would have been closer to 80; others insist that such estimates are notoriously unreliable and that the remains are indeed Pacal's. In 1977, some 25 years after his discovery, Ruz summed up the ongoing controversy with characteristic eloquence. "No matter what we disagree on," he declared, "we are all after the same thing: We want to know all we can about that man in the tomb. None can deny that his reign must have been one of the greatest in all the ancient history of the Americas."

That opinion was based not only on the grandeur of his tomb but also on the myriad wonders of art and architecture throughout Palenque. At least three temples and an elaborate palace complex owe to Pacal's zeal for construction; his son Can-Balam (sometimes written as Chan-Bahlum), or Snake-Jaguar, was equally diligent, completing his father's tomb as well as raising three other major structures, known today as the Temples of the Cross, the Foliated Cross, and the Sun. Sculptured images and glyphic inscriptions abound on the edifices and, most important of all, give a detailed portrait of what mattered most to these two rulers and their people. The picture that emerges has suggested to some scholars that subtle changes in the role of kingship were taking place, and that these changes may offer some inkling of what led to the mysterious plummet of Classic Maya society, at Palenque and elsewhere, from its loftiest perches.

At four different places in Palenque, Pacal and his son erected so-called king lists, dynastic records that traced their royal lineage back to AD 431. Apparently the two were extremely concerned with legitimizing their own right to rule, and the reason seems to be that twice during the city's history a king had inherited the throne through his mother; Pacal himself had done so. Since Maya custom held that hereditary succession was normally patrilineal, Pacal and his son felt called upon to adjust the parameters somewhat.

In the Temple of Inscriptions, then, Pacal had glyphs carved that directly linked his mother, Zac-Kuk, with the First Mother, the goddess who created the gods and first kings of the present Maya universe. Furthermore, the inscriptions relate that Pacal's birthday corresponded to that of the First Mother, implying a personal connection with the goddess. His goal, according to some interpretations, may have been to establish that he had a divine right to the throne that superseded his more problematic hereditary right. As has been seen at other sites, a godly foundation for royal authority was not exactly unusual. Pacal, however, seems to have been making a special and quite personal point of it.

For his part, Can-Balam took the personal element a step further. On each of the three temples built during his reign are long glyphic texts in two parallel sections, with one side recounting events from the creation myth of the First Mother and the other side linking these events to historical occurrences at Palenque, including Pacal's birth, the ritual designation of his son as heir, and Can-Balam's own accession rites—once again a clear effort to legitimize the ruler by connecting him with the gods. But even more significant are some of the carved images on these temples. Scenes inside show Can-Balam in simple dress, facing a smaller figure across a representation of the *axis mundi* ("world tree"), a tree representing the center of the universe; fragmentary carvings on the temple exteriors appear to show Can-Balam in full regal attire. The identity of the smaller figure remains subject to debate, but some believe he may be Pacal, and that the imagery depicts Can-Balam in the underworld of Xibalba—where he was thought to go whenever he went inside a temple to perform bloodletting—receiving kingly power directly from his dead father; he then returns to this world, represented by the outside walls, as the new ruler.

Whatever the precise meaning of the imagery—some scholars think the smaller figure is the young Can-Balam at the time of his designation as heir—there can be no mistaking that both son and father had gone to great lengths to emphasize their importance as individuals. This is especially true if the tablets show what the epigrapher Linda Schele calls the "direct transmission of the sacred essence of royal power" between the two. They almost seemed to be saying that a dynasty depended not merely on family connections but on a degree of personal prestige as well. Indeed, some of the carvings in the Temple of the Sun show Can-Balam dressed as a warrior, calling attention to his role as a fighter for his kingdom and perhaps reminding the people of how he may have proved himself in battle.

Did all this have implications for the ultimate collapse of the Maya? At Palenque, for example, things seem to have fallen apart a little more than a century after Can-Balam's time. In the search for answers, scholars have turned to other sites that were flourishing during this period, uncovering more great stories of kings and their domains—and occasional signs of possibly fateful developments.

Alberto Ruz's find at Palenque, with its revelation of just how

Painted soon after the 1946 discovery of the city of Bonampak, 80 miles southeast of Palenque, this watercolor copies one of several magnificent murals decorating one of the site's largest buildings—images that challenged scholars to reconsider their view of the Maya as a peaceful people. Here, scenes of events occurring between AD 790 and 792 show loincloth-clad prisoners of war suffering torture and decapitation at the feet of Bonampak's finely dressed lords and ladies.

prestigious Maya kings were, followed on the heels of an equally startling discovery at Bonampak, another great city of the Classic period that lay about 80 miles to the southeast. Remarkably well preserved painted murals inside a temple showed vivid scenes of bloodletting, war, and sacrifice *(opposite),* all performed in commemoration of the king's presentation of his son to the people as heir to the throne. Scholars at the time were shocked, having had little prior knowledge of such practices among the Maya, and they now began to think of these people as particularly cruel and bloodthirsty. There was obviously a violent side to Maya life, as there is to almost every culture's. But viewed in the proper context, these apparent barbarities have since been understood as essentially holy, reverent acts by the Maya, designed to help maintain the cosmic order and playing a significant role in kingship. However, one question facing modern investigators trying to fathom what happened to the Maya is whether such carefully orchestrated and managed violence as ritualized warfare—in which the prime goal was the capture of prisoners for sacrifice—had gotten out of hand, and if so, why.

Archaeologists pursuing the story of the last days of the Maya golden age have come upon especially fascinating details at Copán, one of the most striking sites of the entire period. The lush valley of the Copán River had been settled as early as 1100 BC, and the people there had thrived for centuries. Mysteriously, for about 450 years beginning in 300 BC, a period when cities such as Cerros, El Mirador, and Tikal were rising to prominence, building virtually came to a halt in the Copán valley and settlements were largely abandoned. The area recovered shortly thereafter, and the city known as Copán began to take shape, growing more elaborate over the next 600 years.

At its heart was a soaring man-made acropolis in three parts topped with stunningly detailed temple-pyramids and numerous carved steles. The centerpiece of the plaza at the foot of the Main Acropolis was a white temple dating to the eighth century AD, highlighted by sculptures that had been painted red and perhaps other colors, and featuring a stairway of carved stone. Each of the 72 steps was embellished with hieroglyphs—the single largest sample of Maya writing known to exist. Even in ruins, the site remains one of the most impressive groupings of art and architecture in the Americas.

Unlike most of the other great Maya cities, however, Copán suffered from a regional scarcity of limestone for use in the building of its sacred and residential structures. The little lime that was avail-

able was reserved for use as a protective plaster coating to seal floors and exterior surfaces; for basic mortar, workers were forced to rely heavily on plain mud to bind together blocks of a greenish volcanic tuff. As a result, Copán's exquisite edifices have fared poorly over the centuries, even though the tuff itself has proved to be more durable than the limestone blocks employed at other sites. Prior to restoration, most of the buildings were in a state of collapse, damaged by earthquake, erosion, and the intrusions of tropical vegetation.

The site has thus posed a daunting challenge to modern archaeologists. William and Barbara Fash and Rudy Larios, cofounders of an excavation and restoration effort known as the Copán Acropolis Archaeological Project, form the core of a group of prominent scholars that continue to be intrigued by the city's legacy of ruins. They have had to sift through more than 30,000 sculptural fragments—"the largest jigsaw puzzle in Mesoamerica," according to William Fash—in their attempts to reconstruct the facades of temples. In 1987, Fash noted that investigators who preceded them had unwittingly added to the difficulties. "We find pieces from maybe five or six buildings thrown in one heap by earlier archaeologists who figured it was an impossibility and gave up. The Maya wanted to make a statement with every temple, so no two are alike. We're working our way through the piles, understanding each temple individually." By 1992, they had rebuilt four.

One structure among the best restored is the ball court, which includes several sculptures in the shape of

Taken in Copán in 1895, the photograph at right shows hoist and pulley at work as archaeologists begin the nearly century-long chore of piecing together the stones of the Hieroglyphic Stairway, so named for its 1,250 glyphs recounting the history of the Copán dynasty. In the inset, modern archaeologists are seen reassembling some of the glyphs.

macaw heads, a royal symbol apparently unique to Copán. Scholars are still unsure of the precise rules of the game played there and at other similar courts throughout Mesoamerica. Ceramic paintings suggest that players hit a heavy rubber ball using only their hips and buttocks, bouncing the ball off the sloped surfaces that formed the sides of the court and keeping it from touching the central floor. At times, it seems, the game was played for the highest of stakes, and defeat meant death by sacrifice. Some carved reliefs indicate that a captive noble or king might even be trussed up in a helpless knot to serve as the ball, being batted around the court until his back broke. Such occasions, however, were no doubt relatively rare or they would not have been specially memorialized in stone.

Even the more routine contests were likely viewed as far more than mere sport, serving as a form of ritual combat in which the dramas of the Maya religious pantheon were played out. After all, the Hero Twins themselves had battled the Lords of the Underworld in a ball game. By sponsoring the game, and perhaps even participating in it, the ruler was seen to be helping to ensure the continued movements of the sun, the moon, and other heavenly bodies.

An arena of bloody sport for some 400 years, the ball court at Copán—shown restored here—occupies the southern end of the great ceremonial plaza next to the Hieroglyphic Stairway, which rises up the face of a 90-foot-high pyramid. Stone figures representing Copán's rulers are spaced along the center of the stairway.

Copán's many inscriptions and steles indicate that the city enjoyed the rule of a single dynasty for more than 400 years beginning in the fifth century AD, a factor that contributed greatly to its development as a major power. One of the most important monuments, known to scholars as Altar Q, sits at the base of a massive pyramid built toward the end of the eighth century by Copán's last king. On its four sides, the stone altar presents detailed portraits of the 16 members of the dynasty. Dressed in royal regalia, each sits cross-legged upon a glyph that bears his name. Ever concerned with the connection to ancestral roots, the 16th ruler, builder of both pyramid and altar, shows himself face to face with the founder of the line, completing the dynastic circle.

That first king, Yax-Kuk-Mo', or Blue-Quetzal-Macaw, came to power in AD 426, according to a date on the altar and on a stele commemorating a later ruler. He apparently supervised the construction of the first of Copán's major temples and presided over the city's rebirth after its mysterious abandonment. Although technically not the first ever to hold power there, he had evidently demonstrated sufficient prestige—and, perhaps, personal charisma—to be recognized by all subsequent rulers as the founder of their line. He was, according to William Fash, the "George Washington of Copán."

One of the longest-lived of his 15 descendants was the dynamic Smoke-Jaguar, who took the throne in 628 and reigned for 67 years. Celebrated as the Great Instigator, Smoke-Jaguar led Copán through a period of unprecedented growth, expanding its dominion farther than ever before—possibly through the kind of territorial warfare that had seen Tikal lay claim to Uaxactún. The nobility that served under him likely governed in conquered cities, as Smoking-Frog had for Great-Jaguar-Paw. Thousands of new settlers may have flowed into the Copán region during his tenure, the population perhaps increasing to as many as 10,000. The land surrounding the acropolis became choked with new temples and residences for the elite, while in the outlying districts trees were felled and fields that had long been used for corn production were abandoned to make room for the swelling population. The peasantry was pushed outward, and as more and more of the arable land was consumed, some farmers were reduced to tilling the inhospitable slopes of mountainsides.

GETTING TO THE HEART OF A MYSTERY

"Anything this grand must be the tomb of a king," mused William Fash, director of the Copán Acropolis Archaeological Project, when he beheld a burial crypt secreted deep in the bowels of Structure 26, the pyramid that supports the magnificent Hieroglyphic Stairway. It was a good hunch: Inside the chamber lay a skeleton surrounded by a stunning array of treasures reserved exclusively for the elite and attended by the bones of a 12-year-old boy apparently sacrificed during the funeral event. But who actually was buried here?

In assembling clues to the occupant's identity, the physical anthropologist Rebecca Storey confirmed that the remains belonged to a man who had led a life free of

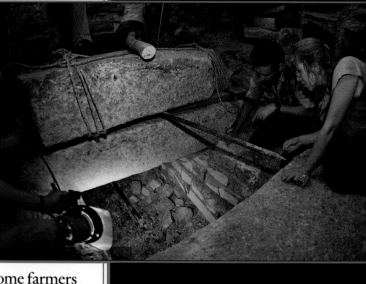

Searching for clues to the identity of the tomb occupant, project director William Fash examines an array of grave goods lying just as they were found. The green balls are jade, once part of a necklace. The earrings (above), measuring some two and a half inches in length, are also jade.

hard labor and degenerative disease. But the idea that he had once ruled Copán evaporated when Storey revealed his age at death as between 35 and 40—at least 20 years too young to be either 18-Rabbit or Smoke-Jaguar, sole rulers during the era in which the tomb was built. However, among the grave goods of jade, spiny oyster shells, and ceramics *(overleaf)*, the team found other clues: a collection of paint pots and a vessel decorated with an image of a scribe or perhaps the patron god of scribes during the Classic era.

Project artist and sculpture coordinator Barbara Fash—who reassembled thousands of tumbled down and broken works at Copán—peers expectantly inside the coffin as one of its 11 massive capstones, made of volcanic rock, is lifted for the first time.

In 16th-century AD Yucatan the scribe's office—an esteemed one involving the writing of historical accounts, ritual texts, and land documents, among other things—was held by a younger son in the royal family. If this was true earlier, the tomb likely enshrined not a king but a king's second son—probably that of Smoke-Jaguar, Copán's greatest ruler.

Discovered in the tomb, a small pot brimming with desiccated red pigment and a dish showing the face of a scribe, his net cap, and paintbrush helped archaeologists deduce not only the occupation but also the probable identity of the tomb's occupant.

From fragments such as those at left, found scattered outside the royal scribe's burial vault in the Hieroglyphic Stairway pyramid, archaeologists restored these clay effigies—four out of a total of 12—to their former regal glory. They speculate that the half-size figures represent all rulers who had governed Copán

Smoke-Jaguar's grandioseness spread well beyond the confines of the city. Tradition held that the summits of pyramids or plaza courtyards were specially designated as the ceremonial stages for kings, the settings for their mystical unions with the spirit world. Smoke-Jaguar proceeded on a far grander scale. During his reign he erected a series of steles throughout the valley that marked the whole of Copán as his personal sacred space. In this way the king declared that the entire region served as his portal to the otherworldly region of the gods.

This royal hubris was to exact a terrible toll on his successors. When his son, 18-Rabbit, assumed power in 695, Copán continued to expand. The new king, known in complementary fashion to his father as the Great Integrator, did his best to consolidate these gains. At the peak of his 43-year reign, 18-Rabbit controlled an area of well over 100 square miles, and many non-Maya from the surrounding territories were doubtless drawn into the community. Among 18-Rabbit's projects was the construction of a pair of causeways that connected the city's core with the outlying settlements; he also oversaw the creation of a splendid gallery of art and sculpture celebrating the dynasty. A veritable army of architects, sculptors, and scribes must have worked to transform the center of Copán into a flamboyant expression of Maya royal power. "His reign," says William Fash, "may well have marked the culmination of sculpture and hieroglyphic writing at Copán."

Such an ambitious scheme was intended to emphasize the belief that the king was not only the ruler of Copán but also a central figure in the workings of the universe itself. In truth, however, 18-Rabbit's lavish displays may have betokened an underlying insecurity. There are indications that members of the Copán elite were no longer convinced of the king's absolute divine authority: Some monuments and steles, for example, were erected to the glory of individual nobles. Availing themselves of the finest artisans and materials, these nobles even appropriated symbols and forms once reserved exclusively for the king.

As it happened, a restless upper class proved to be the least of 18-Rabbit's troubles. Toward the end of his reign, he faced a far more immediate threat when jealous rivals rose up against him. During his father's rule, a minor neighboring town called Quiriguá had been under the hegemony of Copán. In keeping with his duties as liege lord of the small domain, 18-Rabbit presided there in the year 725 over the installation of a new ruler named Cauac-Sky. But Cauac-Sky evidently chafed at his subordinate position, and 13 years after his accession he turned against 18-Rabbit. No one knows for sure whether the two leaders actually met in battle, but somehow or other 18-Rabbit fell victim to the ultimate humiliation: He was captured and led back to Quiriguá as a prisoner. There, on May 3, 738, the mighty 18-Rabbit was beheaded at the hands of his former subject.

The death of 18-Rabbit dealt a crippling blow to the Copán dynasty. For a culture that so revered its royalty, the defeat and sacrifice of the king must have been devastating. Presumably already shaken by the discontent of the elite, Copán's royal lineage would never fully recover its lost prestige.

Nevertheless, the successors of 18-Rabbit mounted an aggressive campaign to reaffirm the glory of the Yax-Kuk-Mo' dynasty. The 15th king, Smoke-Shell, who began his reign in 749, attempted to revive the dynasty through a judicious political marriage to a royal bride from the kingdom of Palenque. An ambitious leader, Smoke-Shell completed the construction of the temple-pyramid featuring Copán's fabled Hieroglyphic Stairway. Seen in the light of 18-Rabbit's downfall, the elegant text, which records the accessions and deaths of Copán's first 14 rulers, marks a decided change in tone from earlier inscriptions. As well as equating these kings with the forces of the cosmos, the Hieroglyphic Stairway presents them as battle-hardened warriors with shields in one hand and spears in the other. The inscriptions stress the dangers of the earthly realm and the need for a strong king to combat them. Even the form of the text strikes a menacing tone: The glyphs rise out of the mouth of a Vision Serpent, symbol of a sacred portal to the Underworld, implying that the departed rulers might one day return.

In 1987, the 21-year-old epigrapher David Stuart, then a

student at Princeton University but already well known for his scholarly contributions, discovered a clay pot at the base of the stairway

READING THE SIGNS ON MAYA WALLS

READING THE SIGNS ON MAYA WALLS

In celebration of the 20th anniversary of his rise to power in AD 695, 18-Rabbit erected a beautiful building at Copán—a temple now bearing the innocuous name Structure 22. Its commemorative purpose was unknown, however, until Maya scholar David Stuart (below) decoded the hieroglyphic dedication carved into a stone step in its inner chamber. A genius in the science of epigraphy, or of cracking these ancient writings, Stuart—who as a boy traveled with his parents on digs—was deciphering glyphs by age 10 and at the unprecedented age of 18, in 1984, had garnered a prestigious MacArthur Fellowship for his groundbreaking work.

Glyphs accompanying stone

masks at each of Structure 22's corners—interpreted by Stuart as mountain monsters—reveal that the temple represented a sacred mountain. The portal to the inner sanctum, where 18-Rabbit apparently enacted bloodletting rituals, describes heaven, earth, and underworld in an elaborate cosmogram *(below)*. One symbol in the cosmogram, an S-shape long believed to represent blood, has been reinterpreted by Stuart and others to signify clouds, a seemingly radical revision. But the difference is actually a subtle refinement: Offerings were made by burning paper soaked with blood to produce smoke clouds, in return for which the gods provided rain.

This sketch of the carved portal to the inner sanctum—drawn during excavations begun at Copán in 1885—is one of many works completed under Alfred P. Maudslay's supervision that enabled epigraphers to begin deciphering Maya hieroglyphs, so complete was their detail.

containing an extraordinary cache of ceremonial offerings. Stuart, who gained reknown for decoding Maya hieroglyphs while still in his teens, quickly realized that the objects bore testimony to Smoke-Shell's efforts to exalt himself and his ancestors. Buried upon the dedication of the temple in 756, the collection included two pieces of jade—which were already 300-year-old heirlooms at the time of their interment—a flint knife, a spiny oyster shell filled with stingray and sea-urchin spines, and a small measure of ash and carbon. In all probability the spines were used in a dedicatory bloodletting; the ash and carbon residue may well be the remnants of bark paper that had been soaked with Smoke-Shell's blood and then burned.

Of particular interest was a group of three elaborately chipped stones known as eccentric flints. The Maya cherished flint and obsidian, not only because they made sharp-edged tools and weapons but also because they were apparently thought to be formed by lightning striking the earth, which would have imbued them with sacred power. So delicately wrought as to challenge the skills of present-day artisans, the flints discovered by Stuart were carved in the shape of seven human profiles—perhaps those of revered ancestors whose blessing had been sought for the new building.

Unfortunately, Smoke-Shell's enthusiasm for his splendid monument was apparently not widely shared. Instead

of lime or even mud mortar, the builders had set the heavy stones of the Hieroglyphic Stairway and of the entire pyramid facade in a fill of loose, dry earth. Some scholars see in the shoddy workmanship a sign that the laborers were uninspired or that the project had not been backed by the nobility—or that the economy had become too feeble to support such a venture. In any event, within a few centuries, the crowning achievement of Smoke-Shell's reign, which he had hoped would confirm the might of his dynasty for an eternity, had collapsed into a heap of rubble.

Not many years after Smoke-Shell's bold effort to maintain appearances, the entire Maya civilization itself seemed to be in the process of disintegrating. At Copán, as elsewhere throughout the Maya world, the downward spiral is best represented by the breakdown of royal leadership. Copán's final king, Yax-Pac, who assumed power in 763, also tried to reinvigorate the city with a building campaign, erecting a number of new temples and monuments illustrating the strength of his heritage, including the famous Altar Q. One sculpture shows Yax-Pac as a mighty warrior, dangling the heads of slain enemies from his belt like battle trophies.

Some scholars suspect that Yax-Pac's warlike display was merely a false pose, a semblance of might masking a fundamental erosion of his status. They point to archaeological evidence that for some time the Copán territory had been divided into at least 12 jurisdictions, headed by nobles who served as a council of elders advising the king but who were becoming increasingly independent. Barbara Fash, who reconstructed sculptural portraits and glyphic descriptions of these nobles on the Council House (*inset and opposite*) and elsewhere, and her husband, William, have termed this a "decentralized—almost 'derulerized'—approach to government." Kingship appeared to be on the way out, and with it would go the Mayas' best days.

A substantial part of the problem was that when Yax-Pac came to power, Copán was hov-

ering on the brink of a massive ecological calamity. Once the region had boasted the richest natural resources available, including plentiful water and fertile soil, but after centuries of heavy use, the hillside and mountain-slope lands simply could not support the population, which had ballooned to more than 20,000 people. The city could no longer feed itself, and farmers had to clear more and more forest to make room for less and less productive fields; soon an area almost 20 miles wide had been stripped of trees. The result was widespread malnutrition and disease—as is shown by analysis of skeletal remains—affecting as much as 90 percent of the population.

Throughout the crisis, Yax-Pac had struggled to hold the dynasty together, but with so many of his people suffering, he would have found little support for ritual displays of power. In desperation, he presumably offered to share the trappings of royalty, dedicating palaces and shrines to certain important families, but even such gestures evidently did little to secure the loyalty of his disenchanted subjects.

His position badly weakened, Yax-Pac managed to cling to power until his death in 820. A possible successor, known as U-Cit-Tok, claims to have "acceded," but inscriptions do not make clear whether he was actually referring to the role of king: The carved altar celebrating the event was never even finished, indicating that his tenure was cut short in any event. The dynasty that had begun four centuries earlier with Yax-Kuk-Mo' had ended.

Copán itself was also in its final stages, as was indicated by the lack of new construction or signs of extensive habitation in the once-thriving heart of the city. Some families lingered on, refusing to give up landholdings in the valley, or farming a few fertile acres on the outskirts. The archaeologists David Webster and William Sanders of

A standard emblem of Maya royal authority, a woven motif that deliberately echoed the mats on which Copán's rulers once sat, graces the east side of the popol na, or Council House, completed in 746 by 18-Rabbit's successor, Smoke-Monkey. Although the western doorway, whose stones were found leaning against one another (left), *had collapsed during a fire in ancient times, it could be readily reconstructed by following the pattern of stones on the intact facade.*

It took no leap of the imagination on the part of the Maya to see the caves that riddled much of the region they inhabited as entrances to the Underworld. Not surprisingly, they revered them and worshiped in their dim recesses.

Archaeologist James Brady of Vanderbilt University has scouted out dozens of hidden caverns in the Petexbatun region of Guatemala and studied their contents—everything from ritual vessels to altars. Because of the mists that would rise from some of them in the mornings, caves were thought by the Maya to be a source of rain and so were associated with fertility and with the fearsome power of the gods. Several have not been entered in more than five centu-

Pennsylvania State University argue that several thousand people continued to live in the region until at least AD 1000. But the glory days were certainly over. By the close of the ninth century, the center of Copán had been almost totally abandoned. For centuries afterward, the only human presence would be the occasional pilgrim returning to pay homage at a shrine, sometimes pausing to leave an offering atop the crumbling acropolis.

Almost all the other great Maya centers such as Palenque and Tikal would soon suffer a similar fate, if they had not already. By the end of the 10th century, the Classic Maya civilization in the southern and central lowlands had all but vanished from the face of the earth. The disappearance of this magnificent society was, in the words of the archaeologist Robert Sharer of the University of Pennsylvania, "one of the most profound cultural failures in human history." Today, the reasons for its eclipse remain a source of heated debate among archaeologists and other scholars, but most agree that some combination of environmental disaster and armed hostility conspired to bring about the end. Disagreements seem to center on the issue of whether pressures on the environment were the cause or the result of

ries. Brady, exploring one of them, had only to hear the growl of the jaguar inhabiting it to beat a hasty retreat.

The most important cave in the area, now called El Duende—which means ghost or mischievous spirit in Spanish—hosted centuries' worth of worship, judging from the array of ceramics and human bones that carpeted more than 600 feet of its approximately two-mile length. Some of the relics predated the zenith of the nearby city of Dos Pilas in the seventh century AD. So many other caverns honeycomb the porous limestone underlying the area that Brady has been led to conclude that the Maya ranked the presence of a cave high on their list of priorities when founding settlements.

El Duende is actually part of a vast network of chambers and passageways beneath a hill sculpted into a pyramid and is cut through by an underground stream. Mountain, flowing water, and Underworld—each imbued with religious significance—converged to make El Duende triply sacred. Its great importance is evident in the rubble found at the cave's entrance *(left)*. Apparently, around the time Dos Pilas fell—probably at the hands of neighboring states—residents attempted to preserve the sanctuary by dismantling buildings and closing up the cave's entrance with massive fitted stone blocks. Such willing destruction of valuable property to protect a sanctuary not only bespeaks a concerted desperation but also bolsters the belief held by some archaeologists that the entire Maya civilization owes its collapse to widespread violence and anarchy.

political breakdown and increasing conflict. At Copán, a failure of leadership seems to have played an important role, but again no one can be certain whether this was the condition that led to disaster or stemmed from other problems that had already set in.

The archaeologist Arthur Demarest of Vanderbilt University has found dramatic evidence that he suggests sheds fresh light on the question. His startling findings have thrown the world of Maya scholarship into an uproar and have indeed prompted renewed debate over the twilight of the Classic period.

His investigations have centered on a virtually unexplored site in Guatemala known as Dos Pilas, which lies about 60 miles southwest of Tikal. In the spring season of 1991, he and his colleagues had devoted themselves to tunneling into the heart of an eroded pyramid in search of a tomb, much as Alberto Ruz had done at Palenque some 40 years earlier. Their first two shafts had collapsed during the digging, but by April they had managed to reach a level 30 feet below the pyramid summit and had drilled holes through to a chamber below. So unstable was the surrounding structure that they constantly feared for their lives. Later, Demarest recalled the feeling of peering through the holes into the blackness: "I want to shrink up and crawl through. But all I can see is this big rock on top that's going to fall and kill us."

Carefully, however, they were able to enlarge the holes enough to enter what was indeed a tomb. Inside, they discovered the skeleton of a man believed to be in his forties bedecked in a regal headdress of jade, conch, and pearl. Nearby were obsidian blades that undoubtedly served in bloodletting ceremonies, beautifully preserved ceramics, and feasting trays covered with glyphs.

Demarest feels sure that the skeleton is that of the king of Dos Pilas during the early eighth century, a mysterious figure known only as Ruler 2 because his name glyphs have yet to be deciphered. He was one of several rulers who led Dos Pilas on an ambitious campaign of warfare and territorial expansion.

Under the reigns of Rulers 2, 3, and 4, Dos Pilas aggressively pushed its borders outward to engulf roughly 1,500 square miles, briefly making it one of the largest kingdoms in the Maya world. This relentless expansion may have reflected a desire to dominate critical trade routes. As at Copán, however, the rulers could not maintain control, and after the fall of Dos Pilas in 761, the region erupted into conflict. The evidence shows that many of the proud ceremonial centers of this region were converted into battle zones and fortresses, complete with deep moats and hastily constructed ramparts. Dos Pilas itself was surrounded by a series of rough concentric walls, one of which runs right through a former palace and over such structures as a hieroglyphic stairway. The sense of urgency and desperation is revealed by the fact that many of the defenseworks were patched together with cut stone pulled off the pyramids and temples.

Dozens of broken lance points found along the ramparts indicate that the fighting did indeed sweep over the ritual centers. Shallow graves mark spots where farmers fell defending their lands. "As their hegemony crumbled, it all went to pieces," says the Maya scholar David Freidel. "It was anarchy. It became the total chaos that is the aftermath of war."

Demarest concludes that this atmosphere of hostility and the subsequent breakdown of social order led to the environmental collapse that ultimately extinguished this phase of Maya civilization. The way in which the Maya fought their battles having been profoundly altered, the entire area was plunged into chaos, perhaps precipitating a devastating disruption of the local ecology. Although some scholars question the sequence of events, even Demarest's critics agree that the importance of the new evidence unearthed at Dos Pilas cannot be ignored. Without question, the Maya world had descended to a level of violence previously unimagined.

Despite the widespread catastrophe, the final pages of the Maya story were still to be written: To the north, in Yucatan, further glories had yet to unfold. But there was no denying that the Maya had reached the pinnacle of their achievement and would never climb as high again. Where once great kings had ruled from towering pyramids, a quiet and eternal pall had settled.

MIRRORS OF THE PEOPLE

The Maya viewed the world with a combination of dread and wonder. To them, the three levels of the cosmos, the Overworld of the heavens, the Middleworld that was earth, and the Underworld of the dead, were all alive with sacred energy. Cosmic order or balance could be maintained only by reciprocal acts of generosity by gods and humans. In other words, the gods would continue to bestow food, children, sunshine, rain, and other gifts of life on the Maya in return for acknowledgment, respect, and praise. Over time it became the express duty of the nobility or elite, on behalf of their people, to perform the ritual acts of devotion necessary to keep the earthly and the supernatural worlds in alignment.

The development of Maya civilization coincided with the evolution of a highly stratified class system. The royal families, thought to be of divine origin, directed all aspects of community life from cultivation to warfare. At the apex of the elite class was the king or supreme ruler. Descended from sacred lineage, the ruler communicated directly with the other worlds and served as the center of the Maya universe as incarnate god and temporal leader. Although bloodlines were typically determined patrilineally, royal families forged important alliances through marriage, and noblewomen often held high office. And at Palenque, two women attained the rank of supreme ruler.

Clothing and accouterments adorning the sacred person of the king represented more than just accumulated wealth; they signified his supernatural power. The trappings of the Maya nobility as well as of their courtiers and captives are depicted in great detail in ceramic figurines—seen here and on the following pages—from graves on the island of Jaina, off the Yucatan coast. The nobleman and noblewoman above, for example, apparently display prized round mirrors. Emblems of rulership, mirrors symbolized brilliance and power; indeed a great lord was regarded as the "mirror of his people.

A COURTLY EXISTENCE IN ROYAL PALACES

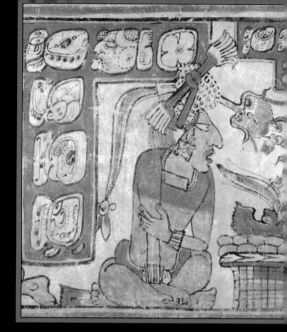

By the Classic period, the Maya nobility were firmly ensconced in their position as hereditary leaders. Although the responsibility to their people was great, the perquisites were many. Social standing accorded at birth determined access to goods, housing, position, and power throughout life.

The layout of a ceremonial city centered around a core area where the elite lived and conducted religious and administrative business, as at Copán and Tikal. There perhaps 100 family members constituted the royal circle, attended by many more courtiers, musicians, scribes, and artisans.

An evocative depiction of an enthroned ruler, shown on the vase rollout below, illustrates some of the amenities of court life. A conch-shell trumpet and two wooden horns blare *(left)* while members of the court, with fan and flowers, await the lord's bidding. Dwarfs, frequent special courtiers, sit at the feet of the bejeweled and head-dressed noble who reclines comfortably against a large pillow, his reflection presumably captured in a mirror held at an angle by a diminutive helper.

Furniture was sparse in the palaces, consisting as it did mainly of built-in benches and platforms and portable tables and stools. Nevertheless, the art, writing, jewelry, textiles, and pottery that have come down to modern times intact reveal a lifestyle that was both elegant and sophisticated.

A Maya lord, seated on his throne, re-
ceives visiting nobles. Each holds an el-
bow with one hand, a sign of respect. The
visitors also show their esteem by offering
a gift to the royal in the form of a length
of cloth, held by the attendant at right.

A nobleman's expansive gestures and res-
olute expression suggest that he is making an impassioned speech, perhaps in the
performance of his royal duties. Formed
by hand and in molds, the Jaina figurines portray not only detailed examples of
elite finery but also the physical features,

MUSIC AND DANCE: JOY TO THE GODS

Music and dance were vital to the Maya, used by them to praise, beseech, and give thanks to their deities. Rites of passage, the call to arms, hunting and planting, and discourse with the gods were all accompanied by appropriate musical compositions and choreography. Although the sounds of the music and the rhythms of the movements have been lost, the performers' presence is ubiquitous in surviving murals, vase paintings, and sculptures of courtly life.

There, musicians play drums, trumpets, flutes, and whistles, and dancers step singly, in pairs, or in groups. Of the instruments used, drums were made from wood, clay, and the shells and breastplates of tortoises; trumpets from conch shells or long gourds attached to hollow sticks; and flutes and whistles from wood and deer bone.

Hunters, carrying blowguns, celebrate the success of their deer hunt by joyously blowing conch-shell trumpets as they make their triumphant way back to the village. Today their descendants have traded their loincloths and blowguns for blue jeans and shotguns.

An elegantly dressed noble couple prepare to dance (below). In this vase painting, the artist conveyed the formality of the pair's movements by raising just one of the woman's heels off the ground, while the Jaina sculpture at left is the embodiment of motion, a lord who has abandoned himself in an ecstatic dance.

111

Predatory birds appear above a howling vision seeker in a ritual depicted on a carved ceramic vessel. The graphic scene includes an assistant (left) preparing the substance to be administered anally by the person at right. Fermented brews of many types were ritually ingested, but datura, made from jimson weed, most often produced the desired visions.

With jug in hand and loincloth askew, this figurine of a nobleman somewhat the worse for drink suggests that formal rituals were not always solemn occasions for the Maya.

The Maya rolled and smoked a number of narcotic plants, as is illustrated by a vase painting of a noble whose cigarette sports a glowing ash. Native wild tobacco, much stronger than cultivated varieties, not only was smoked but was used as snuff,

VISION QUESTS: INTO THE SPIRIT WORLD

As the sacred conduits between the living, the gods, and ancestors, Maya royalty performed a variety of ritual acts designed to open the portals between the earthly world and those of the spirits. In the rituals, celebrants sought to achieve an altered state of consciousness accompanied by visions in which they experienced direct contact with the supernatural. The nobles employed intoxicating brews and plants—some of them hallucinogenic—as a means of inducing visions, but also used them to achieve a condition preliminary to the most important ritual practice: bloodletting.

To the Maya, occasions appropriate for bloodletting were manifold. Every significant event from birth to death, from the planting of corn to the accession of kings required the offering of blood. More than a symbolic act, bloodletting was an opportunity for humans to present to the gods the most valuable gift they possessed.

The figure at right is engaged in a bloodletting ritual. His headdress, earflares, and hipcloth mark him as a noble of high rank, but he wears the rope of a captive as a penitential gesture. Piercing his genitals (the tongue and earlobes were also used in such rites), he allows the blood to drop onto sheets of bark paper. The soaked paper was then burned, transformed into clouds of smoke that the gods took in as sustenance.

The flamboyant attire worn by two ball-playing nobles on a painted vase rollout indicates that their game was ceremonial

in nature. It was no less dangerous for being so, however, and both players wear ball deflectors, probably of wood and

leather, around their middles for protection from the impact of the ball, which weighed approximately eight pounds.

A CONTEST OF LIFE AND DEATH

The Classic Maya ball game, as played by the elite, was not an innocuous pastime of a summer afternoon. On the meticulously constructed ball courts tucked in among the major ceremonial structures of a city, participants reenacted the myth of the Hero Twins' grudge match with the Underworld's Lords of Death. And, as in the myth, which recounts the battle between life and death, the outcome of the ritual game may on occasion have resulted in the sacrifice of the defeated.

Details of how the game was played are not known, but Maya art portrays the players in great detail. Heavy padding covered the arms, knees, and midsections of the participants to protect them from the blows of the basketball-size solid rubber ball. The static poses favored by Maya artists nevertheless manage to convey the intensity needed to keep the ball in play. Here, one participant is shown in a defensive stance, and a second player is depicted crouched on the floor of the paved court to prevent the ball from hitting it.

Although for many years archae-ologists were loath to believe that the ball game contained elements of sacrifice, Maya art and inscriptions indicate that the games sometimes ended in death. Captives, in some cases identified in glyphs by name and rank, were pitted against other prisoners or a home team of nobles. Representations of the game's bloody ending vary: A loser could be pummeled to death with the heavy ball, decapitated, or, in a sequel to the game, used as the ball itself, bound tightly and tossed down the temple steps or batted around the court.

A noble ballplayer evinces dignity in repose and a meditative quality at odds with the violence of his sport. Wearing a jaguar-hide hipcloth, his right hand grasps a handstone. The Maya played several different ball games, and this piece of equipment, whose function is unknown, doubtless was used in one of them.

In contrast to the figurine at left, this ballplayer wears none of the standard ball-game costume. Except for the ball in his hand, he is dressed in the simple garb of a captive. The combination of symbolism—apparent beads of blood on the face, a cloth over one arm, cropped hair, and injured nose—implies that the figure has lost the game and may lose his life.

THE KINGLY DUTY
OF MAYA WARFARE

Lack of evidence of extensive conflict or fortifications led early-20th-century archaeologists to conclude that the Maya, unlike the Aztecs, led a peaceful, utopian existence. Closer examination of Maya art and literature subsequently suggested a society committed not just to combative ball games but also to frequent warfare and human sacrifice. Usually conducted in ritualistic fashion, Maya military campaigns were characterized throughout much of the culture's history by elaborate preparations, short battles, and large numbers of prisoners brought home alive.

A period of intense ritualistic activity invoking the gods for assistance preceded each attack. War-

riors then arrayed themselves in magnificent battle dress—plumed headdresses, jaguar-hide clothing, ornate jewelry, pendants, and other symbolic ornamentation. Weapons, on the other hand, were simple and functional, mainly spears, knives, clubs, and shields.

With the emphasis placed on capturing the enemy rather than killing him on the battlefield, Maya kings, who fought alongside their soldiers, relied on strategy and trickery as much as brute force for success. While commoners became the slaves of the victors, elite captives were stripped of their finery and displayed, mutilated, before being sacrificed to the Maya gods, presumably for the good of all.

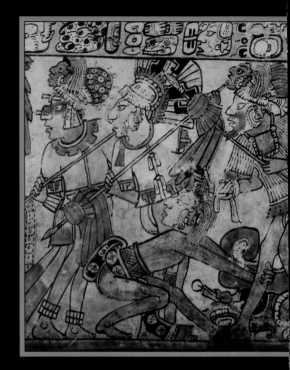

A lord prepares for war with the help of a noblewoman and her attendant. The woman offers the warrior a trophy head *while her servant holds his shield. Glyphs above her head read "cacao vessel," suggesting that the pot was used to hold ca-* *cao beans or a chocolate drink. The piece may have been created to accompany the lord to his grave and the afterworld.*

Carrying spears and wearing impressive battle garb studded with trophy heads, Maya soldiers of the Classic period engage in warfare. A prisoner (left) grabs the leg of a captor who holds him fast by the hair in the standard representation of defeat, and looks back imploringly toward his compatriots.

A victim of captive sacrifice (two views, below) emits an eternal howl of unimaginable pain. He has been scalped, disemboweled, and his hands and feet have been mangled. To finish the job, the wood bound to his back may then have been set on fire.

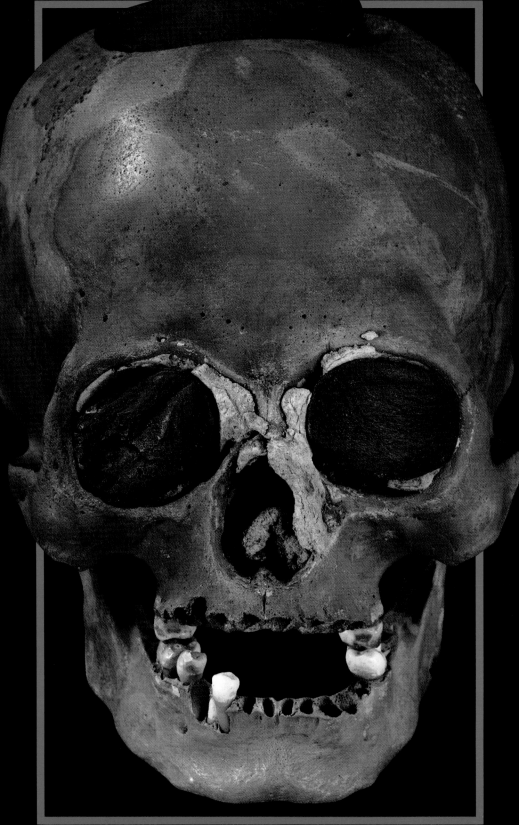

YUCATAN, WHERE THE LUCKY DAYS RAN OUT

Down through the centuries, an aura of mystery and evil had clung to the sacred well at Chichén Itzá, one of the most haunting sites in all the lands of the Maya. When John Lloyd Stephens came upon it during his travels in Yucatan, he could barely stifle a feeling of revulsion as he stared into the natural limestone pit at the oval of dark green, clouded water some 65 feet below him. Stephens, whose descriptions of Maya sites were justly hailed for their fastidious devotion to detail, wanted nothing to do with the notorious *cenote,* or sinkhole, brushing it off in a single arms-length paragraph. Of a type common in Yucatan, the well, which measures nearly 200 feet across, was "the largest and wildest we had seen," he wrote, "with cragged, perpendicular sides, trees growing out of them and overhanging the brink, and still as if the genius of silence reigned within. A mysterious influence seemed to pervade it, in unison with the historical account that the well of Chichén was a place of pilgrimage, and that human victims were thrown into it in sacrifice."

Tales of such practices had first surfaced in the 16th century, not long after Spaniards arrived in the New World. "Into this well," Bishop Landa wrote in his chronicle of Maya life, "they have had the custom of throwing men alive, and they believed that they did not die though they never saw them again." Another Spanish report noted

Amateur archaeologist Edward Thompson's daring foray into the Well of Sacrifice brought to light this censer fashioned from the skull of a young male, still bearing traces of incense after 400 years of submersion.

Tatiana Proskouriakoff's drawing of Chichén Itzá as it appeared ca. AD 1100 emphasizes the importance of the Sacred Cenote (Well of Sacrifice) in relation to the city's ceremonial center. A causeway connects the well (left foreground) *with the plaza containing the Temple of Kukulcan, also known as El Castillo.*

that Maya lords had hurled women "belonging to them" into the well with instructions to find out from the gods below whether the forthcoming year would be a good one; human sacrifices were apparently also made in times of famine, plague, or drought to appease the appropriate deities. But one feature in particular of Landa's account piqued the interest both of his contemporaries and of later explorers as well: "They also threw into it many other things, such as precious stones and things that they prized. And so if this country had gold, it would be this well that would have the greater part of it, so great was the devotion which the Indians showed for it."

The Sacred Cenote, or Well of Sacrifice, as the Spaniards called it, thus promised a twofold bonanza for anyone bold and enterprising enough to attempt to plumb its secrets: the possibility not only of confirming or refuting the stories of sacrifice but also of acquiring more tangible rewards. The first to try was the Frenchman Désiré Charnay, who traveled extensively throughout the lands of the Maya in the late 19th century. He arrived at Chichén Itzá in 1882 with two dredges and a plan for removing the mud and silt that filled the bottom 30 feet of the well, which lay beneath about 35 feet of water. But Charnay failed to make proper allowance for both the height of the cliff and the depth of the water, and he never got started. Then it was Edward Herbert Thompson's turn.

Thompson was one of the last great amateurs of archaeology. The son of a railway station agent, he was born in Worcester, Massachusetts, in 1856 and educated in business and engineering, but it

Today the Sacred Cenote's limestone walls and murky green water appear much as they did in John Lloyd Stephens's description of them in his 1843 classic, Incidents of Travel in Yucatan. *The remains of a masonry structure on the rim of the well, depicted as a stepped platform in Proskouriakoff's reconstruction, may be the site from which sacrificial victims were hurled into the water.*

was the mysteries of the past that ultimately fired his imagination. His first foray into scholarship, an 1879 article arguing that the Maya and other New World Indians were survivors of the lost continent of Atlantis (a view he later disowned), won him the notice of the American Antiquarian Society in Worcester and Harvard's Peabody Museum. Before long he had persuaded these respectable Yankee institutions to underwrite a vague program for archaeological work in Yucatan, and they in turn had arranged his appointment as U.S. consul in the Yucatan capital of Mérida. He arrived in 1885 to begin his extremely influential 40-year-long investigation of Maya sites, which yielded valuable information about many phases and aspects of Maya society.

Thompson was particularly drawn to the architecturally magnificent Chichén Itzá, which had flourished between roughly AD 1000 and 1200, a century and longer after the Classic-period cities of the south had met their fate. In 1894 he bought the hacienda that contained the spectacular ruins of this northern gem, and immediately began contemplating an exploration of the sacred well. "I thought about it by day and dreamed about it by night," he reported. "It became a mania which would not let me rest." As Thompson saw it, there were three options: dredge, drain, or dive. Draining was out of the question because the limestone around the well was too porous, and the pit would almost certainly fill up again. So it would have to be dredging or diving—or a combination of the two.

He decided to dredge first and dive if necessary later, but

before he could begin he had to raise money, purchase equipment, ship it to Mexico and, of course, learn to dive. He bought a bucket dredge, a stiff-legged derrick with a 30-foot swinging boom, and a hand-operated winch, and studied diving under a Boston mariner named Ephraim Nickerson. In time, he became by his own reckoning "a fairly good diver but by no means a perfect one."

It was not until March of 1904 that everything was ready: the derrick perched on the rim of the cliff, four Indian workmen poised at the winch, Thompson studying a point in the water where a dummy the shape and weight of a human body had vanished beneath the sur-

Workers operate Thompson's dredge at the edge of the Sacred Cenote. Although the mining of the well continued for seven years, producing nearly 30,000 artifacts, still more remained lodged in the mud at the bottom. A 1961 project using more sophisticated equipment recovered another 4,000 sacrificial offerings.

face—tossed from the precipice to estimate where the remains of any sacrificial victims might be found. The bucket swung out over the well and quietly entered the water. A few minutes later the surface began to bubble and roil around the cable as the dredge reappeared; swung back over the rim, it deposited its cargo of mud and debris on a platform. Thompson excitedly inspected the pile of muck and found—nothing. "It might just as well have come from any cesspool," he complained.

The dredging continued in similar fashion for a week, with Thompson daily becoming more anxious and fretting that he would become an object of ridicule. Then one dreary morning what looked like two ostrich eggs showed up in the bucket's load. These were yellowish white lumps of what Thompson correctly guessed was a resin that the Maya had burned during sacrifices. When he heated the substance, an incenselike aroma sweetened the air.

Next to emerge were the first fragments of human bones, a humerus and what appeared to be a finger bone. Soon carved wooden pieces, potsherds, and a piece of jade turned up. From then on, nearly every load bore an artifact—tripod vessels filled with resin or rubber, wooden tools, vases, obsidian knives, even versions of the spear-throwing stick that later scholars would see in Maya imagery. One day the Indian unloading the dredge suddenly leaped backward, pointing at a dark snake with a white-ringed neck lurking in the mud. Looking more closely, they found that it was, according to Thompson, a rubber copy of "a small and extremely poisonous viper."

Finally a skull appeared—intact, bleached white, apparently that of a girl. But even more poignant to Thompson was the subsequent discovery of "a pair of dainty little sandals, evidently feminine, once worn by some graceful, high-born maid. Those more than the bleached skulls and bones, more than any other of the finds, brought home to me the pathos and tragedy of those ancient, well-intentioned, and cruelly useless sacrifices." As the dredging continued, he and his team brought up more skulls and other skeletal remains; Thompson himself said there were "scores," but a later

A diver prepares to descend into the 35-foot-deep waters of the cenote. When Thompson explored the well bottom in 1909, he wore similar gear, consisting of a canvas suit, a 30-pound copper helmet, and shoes with wrought-iron soles. Despite careful preparation and training, Thompson sustained ear damage.

systematic analysis showed a total of 42 identifiable individuals. Precisely half of them were adults—13 men and eight women. Of the remainder, seven were between 10 and 12 years old and the rest younger, confirming Bishop Landa's report that "some in their devotion gave their little children" to be sacrificed. Thompson's finds dispelled the clichéd notion that the victims had been teenage virgins. But there was no longer any question that the Well of Sacrifice had been exactly that.

But what of Landa's eager supposition that treasures of gold had been consigned to the depths? Nine months after the operation began, the first such artifacts, as well as some made of copper, came to light—figurines, miniature bells, rings, cups and a bowl, parts of a ceremonial mask. Gold and copper, like obsidian and jade, were not native to the Yucatan Peninsula, and must have arrived via trade with other parts of Central America. Their presumed value again spoke to how important these ritual offerings at the well had been to the Maya.

Dredging continued intermittently for the next several years. Then, in 1909, Thompson concluded that the dredge "unaided by human hands" could do no more. It was time to dive.

His outfit was the clumsiest of affairs: a waterproof canvas suit

Fabulous feathered serpents and Underworld symbols adorn the eye- and mouthpieces of a trio of gold face ornaments found in the Sacred Cenote by Thompson. Crafted in ninth-century AD Chichén Itzá from sheet gold imported from lower Central America, the embossed designs resemble figures carved on local temples.

topped by a 30-pound copper helmet with a plate-glass face mask. A sponge diver he recruited in the Bahamas served as his diving partner and also trained the Indians to man the air pump that was their lifeline. But as Thompson stepped onto a rope ladder to begin his first descent, his crew's confidence was less than inspiring. Each man, "with a very solemn face, shook hands with me," he reported. "They were bidding me a last farewell, never expecting to see me again. Then, releasing my hold on the ladder, I sank like a bag of lead."

Thompson dropped through water that changed color from yellow to green to a black so absolute that his flashlight could not penetrate it. He was nonetheless thrilled at the realization that "I was the only living being who had ever reached this place alive." For the 53-year-old Thompson, who had dreamed of the moment for 20 years, this was the final fulfillment: "I remember distinctly my sensations as my fingers touched upon curious small objects like coins, small nuts, and rings," he later told a colleague. "When I had collected perhaps 20 or 30 I gave the signal and started upward. Before my diving-dress had been more than half removed I plunged my chilled fingers into the dripping pouch and drew out beautiful embossed rings . . . medallions of gold repoussé and gold filigree of exquisite design and craftsmanship." He had struck pay dirt, a treasure-trove worth far more than its intrinsic value because of its archaeological significance.

The items that Thompson recovered from the sacred well and turned over to the Peabody Museum ultimately proved to be the largest single collection of artifacts ever obtained at a Maya site. Golden masks, a copper disk adorned with delicately carved

F. Kirk Johnson, sponsor of a third major underwater exploration of the Sacred Cenote in 1967, surveys rows of human remains, pottery, and artifacts retrieved from the well bottom. This search of the depths was rendered easier than Thompson's after chlorine thrown into the well temporarily killed off the algae present and clarified the green-tinged water.

figures, a stone carving Thompson compared to Rodin's *Thinker,* wood-and-flint knives and ax heads presumably used in the dispatching of sacrificial victims—in myriad ways, these objects contributed to an understanding of life in ancient Chichén Itzá. The art revealed some of the details of Maya ceremonies and demonstrated the richness of their aesthetics; the metals helped identify their trade routes; cotton fabrics preserved in the mud by the airless conditions gave an idea of what they wore. Furthermore, scholars eventually determined that inscriptions on two jade pieces included dates of AD 690 and 706, indicating that people had hurled into the cenote either long-held heirlooms or looted treasures from Classic-period tombs—or that Chichén Itzá had been a settlement long before its heyday.

The view of Maya history that prevailed in Thompson's time divided the Maya saga into an "Old Empire" in the south that ended during the ninth or early 10th century, and a "New Empire" centered in Yucatan, with Chichén Itzá as its presumed capital. But as researchers learned more about Maya calendrical systems, developed a more sophisticated understanding of the culture's architectural trends, and broadened their archaeological knowledge of the region, it became increasingly apparent that there was no clear-cut division between south and north or between old and new, and that the Maya story had in fact been a continuum. Radiocarbon dating and other evidence showed that several Yucatan cities were occupied well before the collapse of the great centers in Guatemala and Honduras; signs of arts and crafts practiced in the south were also found in northern cities. Most scholars now agree that there was no sudden south-to-north migration upon the demise of such southern metropolises as Copán, Tikal, and Palenque, and that the two regions had coexisted for some time.

But it was equally obvious that there were important differences between the northern and the southern Maya. The northerners, unquestionably the major players in the last phase of their people's history, built a half-dozen large cities in addition to Chichén Itzá—ceremonial centers and regional capitals such as Cobá and Mayapán, and the urban communities of Uxmal, Kabah, and Sayil in the slightly elevated country known as the Puuc Hills. These Puuc cities were almost as close to each other as stalls in a Mexican market—Uxmal, Kabah, Sayil, and Labná, no more than 15 miles apart. The Puuc region of Yucatan was chockablock with such settlements. Stephens and Catherwood, traveling on foot and on horseback, occasionally came across two or three ruined towns in a single day.

Some of the Yucatan cities were linked by a remarkable network of roads, and most were tied together at one time or another by a web of trade routes that extended to the older cities in the south. Archaeologists believe that the northern Maya placed more emphasis on mercantile interests than did their southern relations. The northern Maya also developed a distinctive architectural style and their own historical tradition, preserved in the *Books of Chilam Balam,* the transcribed Spanish-era manuscripts that were in effect community archives. Carved images and inscriptions suggest too that at least some northerners may have had a different form of government from that practiced in the south: rule by a group of nobles rather than by an omnipotent hereditary king.

The Maya of Yucatan may also have practiced a fiercer type of warfare than their southern brethren. Although as in the south details of specific battles are lacking, warriors from Chichén Itzá appear to have fought against those from Uxmal and Cobá, while much later on men from Mayapán attacked and sacked Chichén Itzá. In the final decades before the Spaniards arrived, Yucatan society seems to have degenerated into a festering cluster of more than a dozen feuding political domains.

According to archaeologists, the northerners may have been different because of the effects of an alien intrusion—possibly peaceable, but more likely not. Bishop Landa, for example, was told that Chichén Itzá was once ruled by a king named Kukulcan who had come from the west, and that a people known as the Itzá had conquered and occupied the city. "Kukulcan," as it happens, is the Maya name for the god-king called Quetzalcoatl by the Toltecs, the people who dominated central Mexico centuries before the ascent of the Aztecs. For this reason, scholars assumed that Kukulcan was a Toltec ruler who had taken over this Maya city as part of a general conquest. Indeed, one of the *Chilam Balam* texts gives a date, 987, for the appearance of Kukulcan in Chichén Itzá.

But such precision is misleading. The documentary histories, regrettably, are a mix of fact and myth, and the dates themselves have proved to be especially problematic. In the Classic period and earlier, the Maya had kept track of dates according to the so-called Long Count calendar, which precisely listed each day in terms of how many days, 20-day months, 360-day years, 20-year periods known as *katuns,* and 400-year periods called *baktuns* had passed since the Maya year zero. Because scholars have been able to calculate that starting point as 3114 BC, determining dates is a matter of simple arithmetic. But for unknown reasons, the latter-day Maya in the north had abandoned the Long Count calendar in favor of a more abbreviated system known as the Short Count, which was based on a repeating cycle of 13 named katuns. In the histories, a given date is expressed in reference to the katun in which it falls, but not to which cycle of katuns is in place—just as current dates often leave off the century. For this reason, sorting out exactly who arrived in Yucatan when, and what happened next, is thus more a question of educated guesswork than of precise calculation.

The issue of whether the Toltecs did indeed invade and conquer Yucatan can therefore only be resolved by examining sources other than the *Chilam Balam* accounts. Scholars who have studied the carved figures, bas-reliefs, and murals that adorn buildings in Chichén Itzá and at other Yucatan sites have found abundant evidence of their resemblance to Toltec architecture at the site of Tula in central Mexico. Particular features of feathered-serpent designs, jaguar representations, and warrior figures are common to the Toltec tradition and that of Chichén Itzá. Further, murals at Chichén Itzá depict battles in which soldiers in Toltec costumes defeat warriors who are clearly Maya. What this means is still not certain. Although earlier scholars counted such scenes as evidence of conquest by the Toltecs, many now interpret these as encounters between the more Mexicanized Itzá Maya and those who resisted their expansion from Chichén Itzá.

Maya villagers grind corn, tend pots, and head for work in the fields while what may be enemy warriors patrol the Yucatan coast in a copy of a Chichén Itzá temple wall painting. The presence of Toltec-style feathered serpents above the temple (right) signifies the success of incursion by foreigners.

Unanswered questions about the history of Chichén Itzá have fueled scholarly debate for decades, but there has never been any argument about the city's grandeur. Chichén Itzá's physical extent, estimated at some 10 square miles, its ambitious architecture, and its finely wrought sculpture mark the site as the most important metropolis of the later phase of Maya history. Chichén Itzá was one of the few placenames John Lloyd Stephens knew before he arrived in Mexico, having read what he soon realized were relatively feeble portrayals. The city thus more than fulfilled his expectations, "presenting a spectacle," he wrote, "which even after all that we had seen, once more excited in us emotions of wonder."

Stephens spared no effort enumerating and describing the principal structures: the 79-foot-high Castillo, or castle, as it was named by its Spanish discoverers, with its four precipitous stairways; the great ball court, the largest in Mesoamerica, which the New Yorker identified as a "gymnasium or tennis court"; the Caracol, or observatory, a distinctive round structure that some scholars think may have been used by Maya priest-astronomers *(pages 132-133)*; the Temple of the Warriors, guarded on two sides by a forest of some 200 carved columns depicting soldiers, the intent of which Stephens found "incomprehensible." He may also have gazed at a row of human skulls carved into a platform facade near the ball court and at the numerous chacmool sculptures—reclining figures with bowls on their midsection, where the hearts of sacrificial victims were said to have been deposited. Overall, he confessed to being overwhelmed by both the scale and the artistry of the ancient metropolis.

The ball court especially impressed him. As he so often did in his treks through Maya country, Stephens made note of practically every dimension: the length of the parallel walls on either side of the field (274 feet), their distance apart (120 feet), and the size of the ruined temples at either end of the court. He measured the stone rings that presumably served as the game's goals, 20 feet high on the walls, four feet in diameter, and with a hole one foot seven inches across for the ball to pass through. Stephens referred to a description of the game as played in Mexico City written by the Spanish historian Antonio de Herrera, and noted perceptively that the similarity between the Mexico City and Chichén Itzá arenas suggested "an affinity between the people who erected the ruined cities of Yucatan and those who inhabited Mexico." As was so often the case, he was right on the mark.

USING A SKY FULL OF SIGNS AND PORTENTS AS A GUIDE TO LIFE

Early in Maya history, priests began studying the complex motions of heavenly bodies, convinced they were watching the gods trek across the sky. They came to believe they could pick up celestial signs—messages from the deities—that could warn of disaster, foretell the destinies of dynasties, and identify the right moment for planting crops, marrying, and conducting rituals.

The urgent need to recognize and decode these signs led the priests to develop a sophisticated astronomy. Over time they set down their arcane knowledge and conclusions in codices, of which fragments of only four survive to reveal a system of

As the sun sets at the spring and fall equinoxes, a serpent seems to slither down El Castillo, a four-stairway pyramid at Chichén Itzá (left). The ancient Maya may have considered the play of light and shadow, caused by the sun striking the platforms at an angle (right), a manifestation of the god, Kukulcan, the feathered serpent. Modern Maya have revived the celebration of the occurrence.

Maya fears of solar eclipses are reflected in the above glyph from the Dresden Codex. It shows a sky serpent swallowing the sun under the crossed bones of death.

calendars based largely on the movements of the sun, the moon, and the planet Venus.

Sky watching enabled the Maya not only to work out the 365-day solar calendar but also, even more remark-

ably, to define the lunar month to within 23 seconds of modern calculations. They applied this and other sophisticated knowledge to their arts and architecture.

Perhaps even more important for daily life, they devised an astrological calendar called the Sacred Almanac, which defined a cycle of only 260 days. While scholars debate the basis for this shorter cycle, some archaeo-astronomers suggest that it derives from the average human gestation period reckoned from conception. As a horoscope is used by some today, the Sacred Almanac was used to divine the most propitious days for all kinds of human endeavors.

BUILDINGS AND CALENDARS FOR LORDING IT OVER THE MASSES

Knowledge of astronomy made kings and priests seem to be in charge of the seasons and other life-cycle events. And to enhance their prestige, they built awe-inspiring structures, such as the Caracol at Chichén Itzá *(left)*, which highlighted and dramatized celestial displays.

Once thought to have been an observatory, the Caracol is now believed by archaeologists to have been a temple dedicated to Kukulcan in his guise as the wind

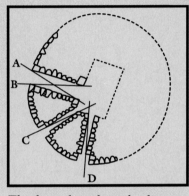

The chart above shows the three surviving Caracol windows, with sightlines of celestial events at the horizon. Line B bisects the setting sun during the equinoxes. The northern and southern extremes of Venus, as it sets, are located by lines A and C. Line D points to the magnetic south.

god. Its architects aligned the windows with positions of Venus and the sun *(above)*. Through the openings, on festival days, these revered celestial bodies would appear as signs of heavenly favor.

The bright planet Venus, rising before the sun and setting after it, was considered the sun's twin and a war deity. Priest-astronomers deduced that Venus was both a morning and an evening star. Accurately projecting the

planet's complex 584-day cycle, they eventually created an almanac combining the solar, Venus, and Sacred Almanac cycles that was probably used for planning battles and sacrifices. This great Venus almanac spanned 104 years, 65 Venus cycles, and 146 gestation periods. With this advanced knowledge, the priests could predict that every 173.3 days, a solar or lunar eclipse was likely to occur—potent magic in the eyes of the ordinary Maya.

Eyes closed, with a noose around her neck, the deity Ixtab, sometimes associated with the moon goddess, may represent an eclipse in the glyph above.

In the Grolier Codex, a skeletal Venus, as the evening star, beheads a captive, indicating auspicious days for war or sacrifice.

The first systematic archaeological survey of Chichén Itzá was a 10-year project launched in 1924 by the Carnegie Institution of Washington, D.C., and led by the respected American scholar Sylvanus G. Morley. Morley subscribed to the idea that it was highly Mexicanized Maya groups, some of them possibly originating in Tula, who invaded Yucatan in the 10th century AD. His colleague J. Eric S. Thompson later argued that the aggressive seafaring and trading people known as the Putun or Chontal Maya, whose homeland was on the Gulf coast in the Mexican state of Tabasco, were the outsiders who transformed Yucatan. He found hints in the imprecise Maya chronicles that "Putun" may have been a geographically based name for the Itzá, the people mentioned by Landa as the invaders of Chichén Itzá, and indeed those who had given the city its full name. Thompson explained the murals showing Toltec warriors overcoming the Maya by speculating that the Toltecs were mercenaries who had accompanied the invading Itzá. The Itzá, by Thompson's reckoning, were carriers of Toltec traditions who introduced that culture's architectural and artistic conventions along with its militaristic spirit to the indigenous Maya of Yucatan.

Although the dates of the presumed Toltec-Itzá incursion are almost impossible to pin down, the current consensus holds that it most likely occurred in waves during the late ninth and the 10th centuries, concurrent with the final phase of the brilliant southern Maya civilization. The bulk of Chichén Itzá's inscription dates fall in

Workers at the Carnegie Institution's Chichén Itzá dig dump rubble from the core of the Temple of the Warriors as they attempt to expose a smaller temple buried within. To keep the larger structure from collapsing, the archaeologists shored up the interior with concrete columns and steel beams.

the late 800s and mention several prominent and apparently coequal lords, including one who seems to have been an Itzá war captain. During the 10th century, Toltec-Itzá power presumably increased, and the city burgeoned with new construction and art in a style that was a hybrid of Toltec and Maya elements.

Some scholars suspect that a number of the other northern cities were eventually overrun by this Toltec-Itzá military juggernaut, which would help explain their apparent abandonment during the 10th century. The *Chilam Balam* chronicles express the sentiment that the Maya never liked their Itzá overlords, even though they may have tolerated and eventually accepted them. The most charitable characterization of the Itzá in these texts is "those who speak our language brokenly"; elsewhere they are described as "tricksters and rascals," "foreigners," and "people without fathers or mothers."

In the early 1950s, Samuel K. Lothrop of Harvard added another piece to the Maya-Itzá-Toltec mosaic in an analysis of several embossed gold disks the size of dinner plates that Edward Thompson had extracted from the muck in the sacred well. One disk shows what appears to be an interrogation scene in which a bearded Toltec warrior questions two Maya prisoners, identifiable by their body ornaments. The captives are seated with their arms bound above the elbows and pinned behind their backs. A second disk depicts a Toltec chief about to hurl a spear at two retreating Maya, while in another, five men in a canoe attack a Maya trying to escape on a raft. Lothrop deduced from the historical record that the disks were fashioned in the late 10th century, but more recently they have been dated about a century earlier, corroborating the notion of a Toltec-Itzá conquest beginning in the ninth century.

Linda Schele and David Freidel have evolved a version of Chichén Itzá's history that incorporates some aspects of this idea. In their scenario, the Itzá moved into Yucatan by establishing trading posts along the coast and then a major port at Isla Cerritos on the north shore of the Yu-

Renowned Mayanist Sylvanus G. Morley, third from right, headed the 1924-40 Carnegie project with style, hiring a Chinese cook to prepare lavish meals for colleagues and visitors and playing phonograph records in the ball court, where the acoustics were particularly fine. A Harvard-trained archaeologist and scientist, Morley was once ambushed by government troops who mistook his expedition for revolutionaries. Several men were killed, but Morley was spared because his nearsightedness prevented him from riding in front of the group.

catan Peninsula. They built their capital 62 miles to the south at Chichén Itzá, and from there began a war with the two other major cities in northern Yucatan, Uxmal to the west and Cobá to the east. In a series of battles over an unknown span of years the Itzá prevailed, but rather than subjugate their Maya foes they absorbed them. Eventually the Itzá created an oligarchical government that the surviving Maya at the time of the Spanish conquest called *mul tepal,* "joint rule"—a council of lords instead of a single king; evidence for this can be found in sculptures and hieroglyphic texts that celebrate not individuals but groups of nobles. This shared power was apparently wielded quite effectively: At its zenith in the 10th to the early 12th century, Chichén Itzá dominated the entire region and was as close to being an unchallenged capital as any Maya city ever came.

Then, at the close of the 12th century, repeating a familiar pattern, it suddenly fell. Unfortunately, the only known source for details of its end is a tale from *Chilam Balam* that quite clearly has more of the mythical than the historical to it. A lord named Hunac Ceel, the story goes, who ruled the lesser city of Mayapán about 60 miles west of Chichén Itzá, jumped or was hurled into the Well of Sacrifice. But Hunac Ceel miraculously survived, resurfacing to prophesy glory for himself. He then went about concocting a bizarre plot to overthrow the city. At the wedding of the lord of nearby Izamal, Hunac Ceel used a love potion

Huge feathered-serpent columns flank a chacmool, a reclining figure cradling a bowl, at the entrance to the Temple of the Warriors. Found in many parts of Mesoamerica, chacmools may have been used to hold human hearts. Chacmools and serpent motifs represent a strong Mexican influence in late Maya architecture.

brewed from the plumeria flower to inflame the leading lord of Chichén Itzá with a passion for the bride. The Itzá leader promptly carried her off, as Hunac had intended, thus enraging the Izamal prince. Reinforced by his new ally from Izamal, Hunac Ceel then fell upon and sacked Chichén Itzá with their combined forces, and the city's Itzá residents fled south.

Although scholars reject the fanciful aspects of the *Chilam Balam* account, they agree that by AD 1200 Mayapán had begun to replace Chichén Itzá as the leading city of Yucatan. Long before its ascent, however, and even before the glory days of Chichén Itzá, the city of Cobá had its moment in the sun. Situated amid five lakes—rare in a region where most surface water drains into the underlying limestone—Cobá lies near the Caribbean coast and is almost as far to the east of Chichén Itzá as Mayapán is to the west. First investigated in the late 19th century, the city whose name means "water stirred by the wind" became in 1974 the target of a major survey led by Mexico's National Institute of Anthropology and History and the National Geographic Society. The evidence that has accumulated since then suggests that Cobá's grandeur was grand indeed.

The city turned out to be a surprise in several respects—in the dates of its heyday, in its size, and in the existence of an intricate road system radiating from its center. Cobá also provides a vivid illustration of the scale of work that remains for archaeologists laboring in Yucatan: It is so large, so complex, and so overgrown that decades of fieldwork remain before researchers can begin to put together a complete picture of the place.

The first of Cobá's surprises was its vintage. Inscribed steles include Long Count dates beginning in the early seventh century and continuing to the year 780. This meant that Cobá was contemporaneous with the great Classic-era cities of the central and southern lowlands, and most likely had contacts with them, a conclusion supported by similarities in their architectural styles and in specific hieroglyphic dates. Researchers have found no signs of Itzá or Toltec influence at Cobá, even though pottery fragments indicate that the site was also occupied in that period.

At its peak, Cobá may well have been one of the largest of all Maya cities. A study of settlement patterns in the area revealed that modest houses surrounding the urban hub extended over some 25 square miles; the population may have exceeded 50,000, greater even than Tikal's loftiest numbers. Archaeologists have identified four concentrations of important buildings, with the oldest, perhaps original site nestled between the two biggest lakes. There are at least two major pyramids, each more than 80 feet high, one with nine terraces and the other with seven. The source of Cobá's power remains open to question. Although ready supplies of water suggest that the outlying farmland would have been productive, there is no evidence of an overabundance of natural resources. One possibility is that its proximity to the sea enabled the city to serve as a middleman in the north-south trade network.

The most stunning find at Cobá was its elaborate grid of elevated causeways—called *sacbeob*, "white roads," by the Maya—that spread from the city in various directions. The longest runs 62 miles almost on a straight line west to Yaxuná, a city to the south of Chichén Itzá that may have marked the frontier of Cobá's sphere of influence. Researchers have thus far counted more than 50 such well-built roads totaling almost 100 miles. They are generally 10 to 15 feet wide and between a foot and three feet high, although one rises 21 feet above the ground at one point. The sides were built up with stones and cemented with lime, and the surface was plastered for smoothness and durability; archaeologists estimate that a total of 1.5 million cubic feet of stones went into the entire network.

The purpose of these impressive thoroughfares is more difficult to deduce, especially for a culture without wheels. They might have formed highways for overland trade, with the goods being borne on the backs of porters. Or they could have served primarily for military or religious processions—or as physical manifestations of political ties between allied cities.

The archaeological record indicates that while Cobá may have resisted outright Itzá intrusion, it declined sometime after the Itzá arrival in the 10th century—perhaps, as Schele and Freidel postulate, because of a defeat in war. The city apparently had some measure of resilience, however: Excavators have come upon structures built in a style common to the 12th and 13th centuries, suggesting that there was enough political organization still in place to launch a construction campaign. But the generally poor quality of these edifices is also emblematic of the waning of power.

Cobá was not alone among northern sites in predating Chichén Itzá and thereby disproving the notion of a distinct break

More than 600 ritual objects, artfully grouped and sealed in a cave for 1,000 years, lie as found by a guide from nearby Chichén Itzá in 1959. The cave of Balankanche (Throne of the Jaguar Priest), like all such caverns, was sacred to the local Maya who worshiped not only their own rain deity, Chac, but also goggle-eyed forms deriving from Mexico that bore a resemblance to the god the Aztecs would call Tlaloc. The goggle-eyed visage appears on many of the offerings, which include incense burners, miniature corn grinders, and effigy vessels of clay, stone, shell, and jade. Carbon-dated to around AD 860, the find suggests the Toltecs occupied the area at that time.

between Old and New empires. Uxmal, most magnificent of the clustered cities in the Puuc Hills region, reached its high point sometime between AD 800 and 950. More than any of the other Yucatan cities, even the spectacular Chichén Itzá, it moved John Lloyd

Stephens almost to reverie. There was something about Uxmal—a sense of ordered spaciousness and solidity, lavish and sophisticated architecture, the vistas afforded by the slightly elevated hills—that thrilled Stephens. His first impression was that it resembled the great Egyptian city of Thebes.

Stephens and Catherwood visited Uxmal more than once, exploring its two lofty pyramids, the immense Palace of the Governor, and the other richly carved buildings with their mosaic facades made of thousands of cut stones carefully fitted together. Stephens clambered in and out of the underground cisterns built to store water because Uxmal lacked cenotes. Ever the astute observer, he noted that the glyphic inscriptions at Uxmal were similar to those he had seen in the south, particularly at Palenque, an observation confirmed by latter-day scholars. And as was his custom, he supplemented his on-site investigation by consulting Spanish histories.

A priest named Cogolludo, he discovered, had left an account of sacrifices apparently still being performed in the 16th century at the summit of Uxmal's 93-foot-high temple, long after the Maya political system had disintegrated. "The high priest," the padre wrote, "had in his hand a large, broad, and sharp knife made of flint. Another priest carried a wooden collar wrought like a snake. The persons to be sacrificed were conducted one by one up the steps, stark naked, and as soon as laid on the stone, had the collar put upon their necks, and the four priests took hold of the hands and feet. Then the high

PUUC ARCHITECTURE: A LASTING GLORY

"If Yucatan were to gain a name and reputation from the multitude, the grandeur, and the beauty of its buildings, as other regions of the Indies have obtained these by gold, silver, and riches, its glory would spread like that of Peru and New Spain," Bishop Landa wrote in 1566. Nowhere does his observation seem more apt than in the gently rolling hills of Yucatan's Puuc region.

Of the many closely situated Puuc cities that flourished in the Late Classic period between AD 700 and 1000, Uxmal, Sayil, and Labná stand out for the magnificence of their site planning and architecture. In these cities are found the defining characteristics of Puuc design—quadrangles of monumental buildings faced with limestone, their doorways framed by round columns with square capitals, and elaborate mosaics on the upper facades.

Uxmal, a city of sweeping vistas and buildings bearing extraordinarily complex ornamentation, represents the apogee of the Puuc architectural style. There the soaring arches of the so-called Nunnery's 74 vaulted chambers open its interior to sunlight, and the 330-foot-long facade of the Palace of the Governor boasts thousands of separate cut stones arranged in mosaic-like geometric patterns. Incorporated within the designs, in dizzying array, are the sculpted figures of serpents, turtles, humans, and gods.

Masks of Chac, a god revered in the Puuc for his rain-making ability, adorn the Nunnery's East Building.

Decorative designs such as these lattice patterns and rosettes may have derived from woven prototypes.

An owl, a bird often associated with night, death, and warfare, perches atop an important symbol of rank, the double-headed serpent bar. The eight parallel bars, akin to scepters, in turn overlie a latticework "mat," the often-depicted sign of royalty. The composition may signify the king's traditional link with the Underworld.

The east wall of the Palace of the Governor at Uxmal epitomizes the harmony and proportion for which Puuc architecture is justly famed. Sections at either end of the building were added using the highest corbeled arches constructed by the Maya, innovatively recessed with striking effect.

priest with wonderful dexterity ripped up the breast, tore out the heart, reeking, with his hands, and showed it to the sun, offering him the heart and steam that came from it. Then he turned to the idol and threw it in his face, which done, he kicked the body down the steps, and it never stopped till it came to the bottom." As scholars now know, the horrific ritual—which was practiced in much the same form by the Aztecs in central Mexico—was viewed by the Maya as a sacred act, but Stephens was appalled at the thought of such "murderous sacrifices."

The architecture, however, never failed to stir his admiration and has continued to fascinate the many other investigators who came after him. Most structures are still referred to by the fanciful names given them by early visitors. One building in the main Uxmal complex was dubbed the House of the Turtles for the string of stone tortoises on its cornice, each with a different pattern on its shell. The impressive Nunnery consists of four ornately carved, many-roomed palaces grouped around a central courtyard. Although its layout calls to mind that of a convent and its exact use remains a mystery, it may have been a grand council house or perhaps a military barracks. The pyramid called the House of the Magician has its own legend, tracing back to an ancient Maya story: A dwarf with supernatural powers was challenged by the Lord of Uxmal to build a temple in a single night or be killed. When he succeeded, the dwarf was instead rewarded with the title of Lord of Uxmal himself.

The Palace of the Governor *(pages 140-141),* largest and most opulent of the edifices, may well have been the home of Uxmal's sovereign (unlike Chichén Itzá, Uxmal apparently was ruled by a single king). This gorgeously appointed dwelling is in the opinion of many the finest work of architecture in the pre-Columbian New World; the archaeologist Joseph Ball of San Diego State University calls it "Mesoamerican architecture's finest moment."

Virtually nothing is known of Uxmal's rulers or of its history. Because there have been no systematic excavations, what little has been learned is drawn from inscriptions or inferred from the architecture. A powerful ruler known as Lord Chac is named in inscriptions on a columnar altar, hieroglyphic ball-court rings, and a capstone in the Nunnery associated with dates between AD 905 and 907. An undated portrait of a lavishly dressed noble on a jaguar throne may be the same royal personage. But interpretations remain difficult, in part because northern texts generally lack the lengthy dynastic sequences and parentage statements common in the south; also, many more of the signs are phonetic and deal with enigmatic rituals, leaving epigraphers guessing as to precise meanings.

The consensus among current researchers is that Uxmal was founded in the late eighth century AD. In a 1990 analysis of the latest findings, the archaeologist Jeremy Sabloff of the University of Pittsburgh points out that it was not until then that the Maya knew to build sufficient numbers of cisterns at sites lacking natural water. He finds no evidence that migrations from the southern lowlands boosted the population in the Puuc Hills, and infers from the nearness of the region's cities to each other and the causeways connecting them that they were political allies, perhaps part of a confederation.

Other scholars have provided further speculations about Uxmal's history. The art historian Jeff Kowalski of Northern Illinois University, who has studied the ruins extensively, finds in such sculptural features as the feathered-serpent and jaguar motifs indications that there may have been a fair amount of contact between Uxmal and Chichén Itzá. His reading of the artistic evidence has convinced him that the two cities were united in an uneasy alliance in the late ninth and early 10th centuries. Lord Chac, he believes, was an old-fashioned autocrat, an advocate of the limited ritualized warfare that was commonplace in the earlier Maya tradition. Kowalski speculates that at first Chac may have negotiated and even collaborated with the more militant and oligarchical Chichén Itzá but that in the end he was no match for the Itzá war machine, and the dazzling glory of Uxmal was at that juncture extinguished for good. Archaeologists confirm that major construction ceased in Uxmal before the end of the 10th century, suggesting that the city's demise followed soon after.

Before that final darkness descended, however, Uxmal and its Puuc neighbors together must have formed one of the brightest constellations in the entire firmament of Maya cities. When Stephens got his first glimpse of Kabah, only some 10 miles southeast of Uxmal, he was stunned by its elegance. The site was at the time virtually unknown, its three largest buildings unnamed; Stephens referred to them simply as Casas One, Two, and Three. Casa One, later dubbed the Palace of the Masks, had a 150-foot-long facade ornamented with 250 rain-god masks arranged in six tiers, each of the masks composed of 30 pieces of mosaic stone. Recent work directed by the Mexican archaeologist Ramón Carrasco has revealed gigantic warrior sculptures adorning the rear of the building. A large arch cut out of the jungle by Stephens's work crew is now believed to have been the terminus of a causeway linking Kabah and Uxmal.

Labná, a mere six miles farther south, was another astonishment. Here Stephens beheld a structure adorned with a row of stucco skulls above two lines of human figures in relief, as well as a 276-foot-long palace decorated with a stone sculpture showing the "huge open jaws of an alligator, or some other hideous animal," enclosing a human head. An Old World tourist visiting Labná in its glory days, Stephens reflected, would have been viewed as a spinner of an Arabian Nights yarn when he returned home.

The Puuc cities, which also included Sayil, have retained the same air of fantasy into the present. Until quite recently, archaeologists had only brushed the surface at Kabah and Labná, isolating an occasional date (879 from a doorjamb at Kabah) but otherwise drawing few clues from the ruins. "You take two steps away from the architecture into the bush," Jeremy Sabloff once remarked, "and you're in the unknown." But mapping surveys and various excavation and restoration efforts have begun to remedy the situation. Scholars now agree that, like Uxmal, Sayil and related Puuc cities thrived between the eighth and 11th centuries and that they subsided around the year 1000. Given the dearth of natural water sources, Sabloff

The Palace of Labná, one of the largest structures of its kind in the Puuc region, was photographed by Thompson in the 1920s (below and overleaf). A grand ruin today, the structure, an imposing 65 feet tall and 440 feet long, was modified several times during Maya times.

speculates that there must have been some kind of centralized water authority ("They couldn't have left it to chance"), but what it was and how it worked remains another Maya enigma.

Not too far north of the Puuc clutch but widely separated from them both in the timing of its rise to prominence and in its physical character was Mayapán, the presumed home of the insurgents who overthrew Chichén Itzá around 1200. While the layouts of Chichén Itzá and Uxmal followed an orderly design in the tradition of earlier Maya centers, creating a feeling of openness, Mayapán was a more shoddily constructed, walled town with a chaotic plan—a tangle of buildings of various sizes linked by narrow alleys. The great temples that were at the core of other Maya cities were largely absent; its main pyramid was a smaller, crudely built copy of El Castillo at Chichén Itzá. Archaeologists estimate that the city contained more than 4,000 structures at its peak in the 14th and 15th centuries, but most of them were long gone well before sustained excavation began in 1949.

Mayapán differed from its predecessors in other important ways as well. According to Bishop Landa, the Cocom family that ruled Mayapán—descendants of the supernaturally gifted Hunac Ceel, the supposed conqueror of Chichén Itzá—maintained power by holding potential rivals hostage behind the six-foot-high city

Similar in style to Labná, the restored Palace of Sayil reflects the beauty of Puuc architecture. Constructed around a rubble core, the palace's three stories contain 50 double chambers, with those on the second floor opening grandly onto a column-lined portico reminiscent of ancient Greece.

walls. "In this enclosure," Landa wrote, "they built houses for the lords only, dividing all the land among them, giving a town to each one according to the antiquity of his lineage and his personal value." These lords paid homage to their captor king by "accompanying him, feasting him, and coming to him with difficult business . . . and spent much time in the amusements to which they are accustomed, such as dancing, banquets, and hunting." The poor farmland around Mayapán was offset by the exacting of tribute from the provinces controlled by the gently confined noblemen. The Cocom further strengthened their position with an army of professional mercenaries from the state of Tabasco known as the Ah Canul, whose fidelity was purchased with promises of military spoils.

Mayapán has been studied more thoroughly than other Yucatan cities, most notably in a six-year project in the 1950s led by H. E. D. Pollock of the Carnegie Institution. The Carnegie researchers discovered that the city wall was five miles long, with an average thickness of 19 feet, and that it enclosed an urban complex of about one and a half square miles; the peak population has been estimated to be about 12,000. Small walls within the city may have been property markers or the borders of garden plots. Unlike most of the region's other metropolises, where the houses became progressively smaller as one moved from the city center to the suburbs, in Mayapán the large homes of the nobility were scattered throughout.

Vast numbers of incense burners found in Mayapán appear to have been mass-produced, a new development in Maya history that signified the emergence of a more sophisticated economy. Maya religious life may have been changing as well: In place of great temples, small family shrines apparently served as the locus of worship. In addition, the Carnegie team came upon the first bows and arrows ever discovered at a Maya site, weapons that probably arrived with Mexican mercenaries. Some Mayanists believe that, cumulatively, the evidence from Mayapán points to the development of a society more mercantile and less religiously devout than it had been in earlier times.

Mayapán reputedly died as it was born, in a bloody uprising. In a rare instance of near unanimity, all but one of the early documentary sources agree that the date was around 1441. Bishop Diego de Landa tells the story: "Among the successors of the house of Cocom was a very haughty man, an imitator of Cocom, and he made another league with the men of Tabasco, and he introduced more Mexicans into the city, and he began to play the tyrant and to make slaves of the poorer people. On this account the nobles joined with the party of Tutul Xiu, and they conspired to put Cocom to death. And this they did, killing at the same time all his sons except one who was absent."

The Xiu family owned land near Uxmal, but rose to prominence at a time when the great Puuc city was already a ruin. Archaeology confirms the historical accounts that Mayapán was sacked and burned: Excavators unearthed charred roof timbers and masonry walls blackened by flames and also found evidence of looting, as well as skeletons of Mayapán residents who may have died in the insurrection. With Mayapán abandoned as Chichén Itzá had been before it, the victorious Xius founded a new capital called Mani—near the Puuc area—which in Maya means "it is passed."

The fall of Mayapán sounded the death knell for the civiliza-

SEEING THE PAST IN TODAY

The archaeological record of the ancient Maya— its art, architecture, and writing—has been described as an embarrassment of riches. Accordingly, scholars have spent much of their professional lives excavating, restoring, and interpreting these magnificent treasures. For a fuller picture, however, archaeologists increasingly are turning to ethnography, the correlative study of contemporary and ancient cultures. Aspects of modern Maya society analogous to past practices are particularly prevalent in religious observances. Yucatec Maya, for example, still evoke rain spirits, or Chacs.

A headdress of monkey fur and brightly colored ribbons signals that a reveler portrays a max, *or monkey, during Carnival. Performers act out the ancient myth of the people of the first creation, whom the gods turned into monkeys as a punishment for their misdeeds.*

A Maya woman weaves a brocaded huipil, *the centuries-old traditional garment of her gender. Her methods, also, date from another time—Maya women have woven their cloth on backstrap looms for more than a thousand years.*

tion that had attained such magnificence in the Central American jungles. Mayapán was the last Yucatan city to hold sway over any of the others; when it collapsed, the confederacy disintegrated into a contentious set of 16 rival ministates, each scuffling for territorial advantage with its own private army. In the recurrent warfare that ensued, towns were continually raided for young men who were drafted as soldiers or dispatched forthwith as sacrificial victims, and fields were burned to starve villages into submission. Art and architecture declined amid the constant skirmishing.

The town of Tulum, perched dramatically atop a cliff above the Caribbean not far from the island of Cozumel, attained a short-lived prominence as a trade center during this period. With a population of no more than 600 at its height, Tulum epitomizes the deterioration of Maya artistry and discipline. Its squat, poorly constructed buildings sagged, columns were crooked, stucco was slapped over slipshod stonework. Stephens, who climbed a steep, overgrown trail from the beach to the ruined settlement, found it notable mainly for the aggressiveness of its mosquitoes and the crumbling, unmortared wall that girded the town on its landward side. The strangely undersized doorways reminded him of a tale he had heard that hunchbacks had built the Maya cities. He abandoned this "abode of desolation and solitude" after a sleepless night.

With the arrival of the Spaniards a few short decades after Mayapán's defeat, the fate of the Maya was sealed forever. A Maya seer quoted in the *Books of Chilam Balam* had apparently predicted the foreign visitation and its ominous consequences, telling the people to "receive your guests, the bearded men, the men who come from the East. On that day, a blight is on the face of the earth." But elsewhere in the holy writings is a fatalistic acknowledgment that the Maya were themselves as much to blame for their downfall as were external circumstances. "There were no more lucky days for us," the text reads; "we had no sound judgment." They knew, before this final conquest, that their glory had already faded and that the ancient wisdom had slipped away. Yet, almost in anticipation of scholars' efforts to resurrect their world, they hoped that one day the voices of the past would be heard once more: "At the end of our loss of vision, and of our shame, everything shall be revealed."

TREASURES OF THE MAYA

Not for the simple sake of delighting the eye but in a higher service to gods and revered kings, Maya artists created innumerable treasures designed for rituals of praise, persuasion, and protection. Molded from clay, carved from stone, shell, and colorful minerals, and often painted with bright pigments, their masterpieces took a range of forms, including mythical, human, and animal shapes. All elements of the design were imbued with spiritual or symbolic purpose. For example, the jade in a mosaic mask placed upon the face of a dead king was thought to confer eternal life on his soul. Similarly, the decorated polychrome plate shown above contains a so-called kill hole at its center, punched to allow the release of the dish's spirit so that it might attend a passing soul in the Underworld.

Without the benefit of metal tools or a potter's wheel, artisans working in clay fashioned works of great beauty and precision using molds or applying coiling,

appliqué, and freehand methods. Stone implements and abrasives were employed to shape not only a hard medium, like jade, but also flint and shell. Tradition determined the framework and even the decoration of most projects; nevertheless, these artists expressed remarkable creative freedom in the treatment of small details. The individual who decorated the surface of the plate above managed to capture, in a few quick strokes, the ineffable grace of a dancer extending his arm as he takes a step on tiptoe.

Indeed, most Maya artwork tells a story charged with action or feeling. The men and women who produced it exercised a style that is naturalistic as well as narrative, infusing their subjects with the energy of ferocity or humor or delicate motion. The result of these anonymous artists' efforts—a broad sampling of which is pictured on the following pages—still delights the eye and serves to bring the long-vanished world of the Maya to vivid life centuries later.

Still showing traces of ancient blue paint, a clay figure of a nobleman wearing an undulating headdress suggestive of a fish bends his knees and elbows in a natural pose that evokes grace and fluidity. This piece—used for burial rituals—comes from Jaina, an island known for its fine sculpture in the round.

Gazing inscrutably out of the past, this life-size mask, crowned with a shark-toothed god, once covered the face of a Tikal king or nobleman as he made his journey into the afterlife. Red conch shell and eyes of mother-of-pearl and black pyrite stand out against a background of gray-green diopside, which contrasts subtly with green jadeite earplugs—all fitted together with exquisite precision.

One of the largest beasts in the jungle, a stag dances across a painted tripod vessel crafted in the "mammiform" style—so named for its breastlike legs. Earlier versions of the design, which originated in Guatemala's highlands, were monochromatic; here the artist embellished the container with red, orange, and black, and even inserted tiny clay balls into the legs so that it rattled when shook.

An earthenware container in the shape of
a heels-over-head diving god shows the
influence of other Mesoamerican cultures
on late Maya art with its jaguar spots
and colorful facial stripes. The deity is
thought to be the corn god; he is holding
tamales made from the Maya staple.

A profusion of images envelop this "dark side" of an exotic Maya clay vessel, where a pair of anthropomorphized Vision Serpents face each other below a crocodile-like Celestial Monster. To achieve the complex effects of shadow and depth, the artist used the appliqué technique of cutting pieces of clay and applying them, layer upon layer, to the surface of the jar.

Crafting a tribute to both the real and the symbolic, the sculptor of this dog made of shell—measuring less than two inches long—positioned the animal crouching and panting and inlaid the piece with jade. Discovered in the central Maya lowlands, the ornament dates to sometime between AD 300 and 600.

Conjuring the descent into death, this delicately chipped eccentric-flint master-piece measures 16 inches long. The gaping visage of the Celestial Monster—escort to the Underworld—appears to plunge downward, dragging with it the "sinking canoe of life." On board, three passengers, the deceased and a pair of flanking attendants, convey the powerful force of the dive in their arching backs.

Using the Teotihuacan fresco technique of applying paint to a wet stucco surface, a Maya artist rendered the bright, long-lasting images of a human emerging from the beak of a quetzal on this tripod container. A sculptured head of what may be a god or a spirit rises from the center of the lid and functions as a knob—a feature shared by many other vessels crafted by the imaginative Maya.

Prominent fangs and a throat tinted red with cinnabar add realistic drama to this dog's-head sculpture—in actuality a vessel that can be propped on three tiny feet set into the animal's neck—found in the grave of a Copán dignitary. According to Maya belief, canines symbolized survival and guided the newly dead through the fearsome Underworld.

THE UNRIVALED SWEEP OF MAYA CENTURIES

Just after the end of the last Ice Age, about 10,000 years ago, the first people to inhabit what is now Latin America moved from the north into the lands that would later compose the realm of the Maya—a diverse expanse of highlands and lowlands, thick forests, and scrubby terrain encompassing the entire Yucatan Peninsula, all of Guatemala and Belize, and parts of Mexico, Honduras, and El Salvador. Over the next 6,000

THE PRECLASSIC PERIOD
1500 BC-AD 250

STONE MASK

As early inhabitants became more adept at cultivating and improving food crops, densely populated villages began to pepper the Maya highlands and lowlands. Around 1000 BC, villagers at Cuello in northern Belize were already making pottery and burying their dead in ceremonial fashion, placing bits of jade and other valued objects in the graves. Early Maya art shows the influence of the Olmec civilization—an advanced culture from Mexico's Gulf Coast with trading links throughout Mesoamerica. Some scholars believe that the ideas of kingship and hierarchical society that began to emerge among the Maya may owe to an Olmec presence in the southernmost Maya area from about 900 to 400 BC.

As Olmec power waned, southern Maya trading centers grew and prospered. From about 300 BC to AD 250, large cities such as Nakbé, El Mirador, and Tikal started to take shape. Sacred and celestial calendars were already in use, and these years also saw the development of hieroglyphic writing, as well as the building of ceremonial temples adorned with sculpted portraits of Maya gods, and later, rulers. Royal tombs from this era often contained elaborate burial offerings, such as the greenstone mask above, found in the vault of a first-century BC Tikal noble.

THE EARLY CLASSIC PERIOD
AD 250-600

COVERED BOWL

By AD 250, Tikal and the neighboring city of Uaxactún were among the dominant economic and political powers in the central Maya lowlands. Society had stratified into a ruling elite and a peasant class of farmers, craft specialists, and other workers. Beginning in the third century, kings—endowed with divine status—erected temple-pyramids and steles carved with images and inscriptions memorializing themselves and their reigns; rituals involving bloodletting and human sacrifice served a dedicatory role. Dated AD 292, the earliest known stele from Tikal commemorated a descendant of Lord Yax-Moch-Xoc, who earlier in the century founded a dynasty that was to rule the city for 600 years. Under that dynasty's ninth king, Great-Jaguar-Paw, Tikal conquered Uaxactún in 378. By this time, Tikal had come under the influence of warrior-merchant groups from the great Mexican metropolis of Teotihuacan, apparently adopting some aspects of their brand of ritualized war.

Sophisticated crafts—such as the polychrome bowl above with a fishing bird atop its lid—and grandiose architecture attest to the artistic excellence of this period. During the sixth century, a mysterious lull set in at Tikal: From 534 to 593, few monuments were erected there.

years or so, the native populations gradually shifted from a seminomadic existence as hunter-gatherers to a more sedentary agricultural life. The fledgling farmers began to cultivate crops, in particular corn and beans, devised a variety of stone grinding tools for preparing foods, and started to organize small settlements.

By around 1500 BC, village building had begun in earnest, marking the onset of the so-called Preclassic period, in which the civilization of the Maya took root. Scholars have learned a great deal about the subsequent flowering of this culture through both archaeological finds and the hieroglyphic texts that embellish so many structures, furnishing a remarkable written history of this extraordinary people.

THE LATE CLASSIC PERIOD
AD 600-900

ECCENTRIC FLINT

THE POSTCLASSIC PERIOD
AD 900-1500

STONE FIGURE

Heralded by a frenzy of new palace and temple construction, Classic Maya culture soared to new heights in the seventh and eighth centuries. Tikal renewed its glory, but several other equally strong centers evolved. In the western Maya region, the city of Palenque flowered during the reign of Lord Pacal, who ascended the throne in AD 615 and was buried with godlike reverence in 683. Under the 67-year rule of Smoke-Jaguar, the southeastern city of Copán also rose to prominence in the seventh century. Although linked through royal marriages and shared cultural features—including similar art styles and religious concepts—such centers remained independent. Intercity warfare was common.

Art continued to flourish as skilled craftsmen supplied the ruling elite with a variety of finely wrought objects, such as the eccentric flint above. Probably carried in sacred rituals, this laboriously fashioned item was found in a dedicatory cache at Copán. Rulers continued to erect ceremonial structures and innumerable steles vaunting their personal prestige. Beginning in the eighth century and culminating in the ninth, however, turmoil pervaded lowland Maya culture. Political collapse struck Copán by 822; the last dated inscription from Tikal is 869.

Agricultural failure, overpopulation, disease, foreign invasion, social revolution, and unbridled war are among the theories advanced for the demise of Maya civilization in the southern lowlands. By AD 900, construction in the region had ceased and once-great cities, many abandoned by their inhabitants, were falling swiftly to ruin. Classic Maya culture continued to thrive in some northern Yucatan centers. Distinguished by a highly ornate architectural style, the cities of Uxmal, Kabah, Sayil, and Labná, nestled in the Puuc Hills, lasted until about 1000.

Around that time, the city of Chichén Itzá embarked on two centuries of prosperity. New sculptural motifs—such as the stone statue above, used as a support in the Temple of the Jaguars—and other architectural features reflected a Mexican influence, possibly that of the Toltecs, who ruled central Mexico before the Aztecs. Collapsing mysteriously around 1200, Chichén Itzá was succeeded by the walled city of Mayapán as the major Yucatan power. Ruled by the Cocom family for some 250 years, Mayapán was destroyed by rival chieftains in 1441. Maya civilization then lapsed into disarray and soon faced an even greater catastrophe: the arrival of the Spaniards at the beginning of the 16th century.

ACKNOWLEDGMENTS

The editors thank the following for their valuable assistance in the preparation of this volume: Anthony Andrews, Sarasota, Florida; Michel Antochiw, Mérida, Mexico; Ferdinand Anton, Munich; Ronald L. Bishop, Washington, D.C.; Bénédicte Bouhours, Paris; James Brady, American Embassy, Guatemala; Emile Deletaille, Brussels; David Freidel, Dallas, Texas; Susan Giles, Bristol, England; Ian Graham, Cambridge, Massachusetts; Nikolai Grube, Bonn; Richard Hansen, Los Angeles; Angela Heartfield, Nashville, Tennessee; Christopher Jones, University Museum, University of Pennsylvania, Philadelphia; Justin Kerr, New York City; Martha Labell, Cambridge, Massachusetts; Stanley Loten, Ottawa; Mary Ellen Miller, New Haven, Connecticut; Manfred Mühlner, Dresden; Arturo Romano Pacheco, Mexico City; Alessandro Pezzati, Philadelphia; Dorie Reents-Budet, Durham, North Carolina; Merle Greene Robertson, San Francisco; Karl Taube, Riverside, California.

PICTURE CREDITS

The sources for the illustrations in this volume are listed below. Credits from left to right are separated by semicolons; credits from top to bottom are separated by dashes.
Cover: Dumbarton Oaks Research Library and Collections, Washington, D.C. Background Roberto Schezen, New York. End paper: Art by Paul Breeden. 6: Kenneth Garrett, Broad Run, Va. 8-13: Enrique Franco Torrijos, courtesy Mr. and Mrs. John Plunket. 16: Real Academia de la Historia, Madrid. 17: Luis Arenas, Archivo General de Indias, Seville, Spain. 18, 19: Luis Arenas, Archivo General de Indias, Seville, Spain; Bibliothèque Nationale, Paris. 20, 21: Courtesy of The Edward E. Ayer Collection, The Newberry Library, Chicago—Bibliothèque Nationale, Paris. 22: Bibliothèque Nationale, Paris. 23: Mireille Vautier, Paris. 24: Peabody Museum, Harvard University, photographs by Le Plongeon; third photo from left bottom row from the Manly P. Hall Collection at the Philosophical Research Society, Los Angeles. 26: Courtesy Bristol Museums and Art Gallery, England. 27: National Museums and Galleries on Merseyside/Collection Bristol Museums and Art Gallery, England (3); Gianni Dagli Orti, Paris/National Museum of Anthropology, Mexico City. 28, 29: Archiv für Kunst und Geschichte, Berlin/Museo de America, Madrid. 30: Art by Fred Holz; art by Time-Life Books, courtesy The University Museum, University of Pennsylvania. 31: Art by Time-Life Books, courtesy Linda Schele (first row down, 3); art by Time-Life Books, courtesy The University Museum, University of Pennsylvania. 32: Courtesy Yuri Valentinovich Knorozov, Doctor of Historical Science, Academy of Science, U.S.S.R. 33: Peabody Museum, Harvard University, photograph by Hillel Burger. 35: Neg. no. 330212, photo by Alfred P. Maudslay, courtesy Department Library Services, American Museum of Natural History, New York. 36, 37: Courtesy the Trustees of the British Library, London. 38: Bibliothèque Nationale, Paris. 39: Courtesy the Trustees of the British Library, London. 40, 41: Courtesy Peabody Museum, Harvard University, photograph by T. Maler; Peabody Museum, Harvard University, photograph by T. Maler. 42, 43: Peabody Museum, Harvard University, photographs by Edward H. Thompson. 44, 45: Courtesy the Trustees of the British Library, London; Peabody Museum, Harvard University. 46: Norman Hammond, Boston University. 48: Norman Hammond, Boston University—Lowell Georgia. 50, 51: © Martha Cooper/Peter Arnold, Inc. 52: Lowell Georgia—Eberhard Thiem, Lotos Film, Kaufbeuren/Department of Archaeology, Belmopan, Belize. 53: © Martha Cooper/Peter Arnold, Inc. 54: Bob Greenlee, Bend, Oreg. 55: Mary Elizabeth Chambers. 56: © Justin Kerr, New York. 58, 59: Courtesy Richard Hansen. 60, 61: Eberhard Thiem, Lotos Film, Kaufbeuren/Instituto Hondureño de Antropología e Historia, Copán—Peter T. Furst, Devon, Pa. 62: William M. Ferguson, Durango, Colo. 63: James F. Garber, Southwest Texas State University, courtesy David A. Freidel, Dallas. 64: Art by Stephen R. Wagner. 65: © Martha Cooper/Peter Arnold, Inc. 66: © Justin Kerr, New York; Lowell Georgia. 67: © Justin Kerr, New York. 68, 69: © Justin Kerr, New York, except bottom left, drawing by Michael D. Coe, courtesy The Grolier Club of New York. 71: Enrique Franco Torrijos/Museo Sylvanus G. Morley, Parque Nacional Tikal, Guatemala. 73: Mary Elizabeth Chambers. 74, 75: Enrique Franco Torrijos—William M. Ferguson, Durango, Colo.; drawing by Stanley Loten, Ottawa, Ont. 76, 77: William M. Ferguson, Durango, Colo.; J. & P. VanKirk, Nobleton, Fla.—drawing by Stanley Loten, Ottawa, Ont. 78, 79: Kenneth Garrett, Broad Run, Va.; art by Stephen R. Wagner; Kevin Schafer/ALLSTOCK, Seattle. 80: William L. Fash, DeKalb, Ill. 82: © David Alan Harvey/Woodfin Camp, Inc. 83: Robert Frerck/Odyssey Productions, Chicago—Tony Morrison/South American Pictures, Woodbridge, Suffolk, England. 84: Merle Greene Robertson, copyright 1976. 85: Gianni Dagli Orti, Paris/National Museum of Anthropology, Mexico City. 86: Dr. Arturo Romano Pacheco. 87: Werner Forman Archive, London/National Museum of Anthropology, Mexico City. 88, 89: The University Museum, University of Pennsylvania (neg. no. T4-206c3). 90: Kenneth Garrett, Broad Run, Va. 92: Peabody Museum, Harvard University, photograph by Hillel Burger. 94: Peabody Museum, Harvard University; © Richard Alexander Cooke III. 95: Reflejo/Susan Griggs Agency, London. 96, 97: Kenneth Garrett, Broad Run, Va. 98, 99: William L. Fash, DeKalb, Ill. 100: © Richard Alexander Cooke III. 101: Bibliothèque Nationale, Paris. 102, 103: William L. Fash, DeKalb, Ill. 104: James E. Brady/Petexbatun Regional Cave Survey, Guatemala. 107: Dallas Museum of Art, J. B. H. Henderson Memorial Fund; Dallas Museum of Art, gift of Alfred Stendahl. 108, 109: © Justin Kerr, New York. 110, 111: © Justin Kerr, New York; Lee Boltin, Croton-on-Hudson, N.Y.; © Justin Kerr, New York. 112-117: © Justin Kerr, New York. 118: Peabody Museum, Harvard University, photograph by Hillel Burger. 120: Peabody Museum, Harvard University, photograph by Hillel Burger/drawing by Dr. Tatiana Proskouriakoff. 121: J. & P. VanKirk, Nobleton, Fla. 122: Peabody Museum, Harvard University. 123: Peabody Museum, Harvard University, photograph by A. Tozzer. 124: Peabody Museum, Harvard University, photograph by Hillel Burger. 125: From *The Well of Sacrifice,* by Donald Ediger, Doubleday & Co., Garden City, N.Y., 1971, © 1971 Expeditions Unlimited, Inc. 128, 129: Peabody Museum, Harvard University, photograph by Hillel Burger. 130, 131: Background © 1992 Gary Braasch, Portland, Oreg. From *Codex Dresdensis,* Sächsische Landesbibliothek, Dresden, photograph by ADEVA Bildstelle, Graz—

BIBLIOGRAPHY

BOOKS

Adams, Richard E. W. *Prehistoric Mesoamerica* (rev. ed.). Norman: University of Oklahoma Press, 1991.

Aveni, Anthony F. *Skywatchers of Ancient Mexico.* Austin: University of Texas Press, 1983.

Barrera Rubio, Alfredo. *Official Guide: Uxmal.* Mexico City: INAH-SALVAT, 1990.

Baudez, Claude, and Sydney Picasso. *Lost Cities of the Maya.* New York: Harry N. Abrams, 1992.

Benson, Elizabeth P. *The Maya World* (rev. ed.). New York: Thomas Y. Crowell, 1977.

Berjonneau, Gérald, and Jean-Louis Sonnery. *Rediscovered Masterpieces of Mesoamerica: Mexico-Guatemala-Honduras.* Boulogne, France: Editions Arts 135, 1985.

Brunhouse, Robert L. *In Search of the Maya: The First Archaeologists.* New York: Ballantine Books, 1973.

Carlson, John B. "A Geomantic Model for the Interpretation of Mesoamerican Sites: An Essay in Cross-Cultural Comparison." In *Mesoamerican Sites and World-Views,* edited by Elizabeth P. Benson. Washington, D.C.: Dumbarton Oaks, 1981.

Carrasco, Davíd. *Religions of Mesoamerica.* San Francisco: Harper & Row, 1990.

Castellanos, Fernando Robles, and Anthony P. Andrews. "A Review and Synthesis of Recent Postclassic Archaeology in Northern Yucatan." Chapter 3 in *Late Lowland Maya Civilization,* edited by Jeremy A. Sabloff and E. Wyllys Andrews V. Albuquerque: University of New Mexico Press, 1986.

Ceram, C. W. *Gods, Graves, and Scholars.* Translated by E. B. Garside. New York: Alfred A. Knopf, 1952.

Coe, Michael D.:
Lords of the Underworld. Princeton, N.J.: Princeton University Press, 1978.
The Maya (4th ed.). New York: Thames and Hudson, 1991.
The Maya Scribe and His World. New York: Grolier Club, 1973.

Coe, Michael, Dean Snow, and Elizabeth Benson. *Atlas of Ancient America.* New York: Facts On File, 1989.

Coe, William:
Excavations in the Great Plaza, North Terrace, and North Acropolis of Tikal (Tikal report no. 14, Vols. 1-6). Philadelphia: University Museum, University of Pennsylvania, 1990.
Tikal. Philadelphia: University Museum, University of Pennsylvania, 1988.

Coggins, Clemency Chase, and Orrin C. Shane III (Eds.). *Cenote of Sacrifice.* Austin: University of Texas Press, 1984.

Danien, Elin C., and Robert J. Sharer (Eds.). *New Theories on the Ancient Maya* (University Museum Symposium Series, Vol. 3). Philadelphia: University Museum, University of Pennsylvania, 1992.

Davis, Keith F. *Désiré Charnay: Expeditionary Photographer.* Albuquerque: University of New Mexico Press, 1981.

Desmond, Lawrence Gustave, and Phyllis Mauch Messenger. *A Dream of Maya.* Albuquerque: University of New Mexico Press, 1988.

Ediger, Donald. *The Well of Sacrifice.* Garden City, N.Y.: Doubleday, 1971.

Fagan, Brian M.:
The Adventure of Archaeology. Washington, D.C.: National Geographic Society, 1985.
Kingdoms of Gold, Kingdoms of Jade. New York: Thames and Hudson, 1991.

Fash, William L. *Scribes, Warriors, and Kings.* New York: Thames and Hudson, 1991.

Ferguson, William M., and Arthur H. Rohn. *Mesoamerica's Ancient Cities.* Niwot: University Press of Colorado, 1990.

Ferguson, William M., and John Q. Royce. *Maya Ruins in Central America in Color.* Albuquerque: University of New Mexico Press, 1984.

Furst, Jill Leslie, and Peter T. Furst. *Pre-Columbian Art of Mexico.* New York: Abbeville Press, 1980.

Gallenkamp, Charles. *Maya: The Riddle and Rediscovery of a Lost Civilization* (3d rev. ed.). New York: Viking, 1985.

Gallenkamp, Charles, and Regina Elise Johnson (Eds.). *Maya: Treasures of an Ancient Civilization.* New York: Harry N. Abrams, 1985.

Hammond, Norman. "Preclassic Maya Civilization." Chapter 10 in *New Theories on the Ancient Maya,* edited by Elin C. Danien and Robert J. Sharer. Philadelphia: University Museum, University of Pennsylvania, 1992.

Harris, John F., and Stephen K. Stearns. *Understanding Maya Inscriptions.* Philadelphia: University Museum, University of Pennsylvania, 1992.

Hawkes, Jacquetta (Ed.). *The World of the Past.* New York: Alfred A. Knopf, 1963.

Hellmuth, Nicholas M. *Ballgame Iconography and Playing Gear.* Culver City,

Calif.: Foundation for Latin American Anthropological Research, 1987.

Henderson, John S. *The World of the Ancient Maya*. Ithaca, N.Y.: Cornell University Press, 1981.

Heyden, Doris, and Paul Gendrop. *Pre-Columbian Architecture of Mesoamerica*. Translated by Judith Stanton. New York: Harry N. Abrams, 1975.

Houston, S. D. *Maya Glyphs*. London: British Museum Publications, 1989.

Hunter, C. Bruce. *A Guide to Ancient Maya Ruins* (2d ed., rev.). Norman: University of Oklahoma Press, 1986.

Jones, Christopher. *Deciphering Maya Hieroglyphs*. Philadelphia: University Museum, University of Pennsylvania, 1984.

Kerr, Justin. *The Maya Vase Book* (3 vols.). With essays by Joseph W. Ball, et al. New York: Kerr Associates, 1989-1992.

Kubler, George. *The Art and Architecture of Ancient America*. New York: Penguin Books, 1984.

Landa, Friar Diego. *Yucatan before and after the Conquest*. Translated with notes by William Gates. New York: Dover Publications, 1978.

Leal, Marcia Castro. *Archaeological Mexico*. Florence: Casa Editrice Bonechi, 1990.

Maudslay, Alfred P. *Biologia Centrali-Americana* (Vols. 1 and 2). Edited by F. Ducane Godman and Osbert Salvin. London: R. H. Porter, 1889-1902.

Mercer, Henry C. *The Hill-Caves of Yucatan*. Norman: University of Oklahoma Press, 1975.

Meyer, Carolyn, and Charles Gallenkamp. *The Mystery of the Ancient Maya*. New York: Atheneum, 1985.

Miller, Mary Ellen. *The Art of Mesoamerica from Olmec to Aztec*. London: Thames and Hudson, 1990.

Morley, Sylvanus G., and George W. Brainerd. *The Ancient Maya* (4th ed., rev. by Robert J. Sharer). Stanford, Calif.: Stanford University Press, 1983.

Morris, Earl Halstead. *The Temple of the Warriors at Chichen Itza, Yucatan*. Washington, D.C.: Carnegie Institution of Washington, 1931.

National Geographic Society. *Lost Empires: Living Tribes*. Washington, D.C.: National Geographic Society, 1982.

Popol Vuh. Translated by Dennis Tedlock. New York: Simon and Schuster, 1985.

Popol Vuh. English version by Delia Goetz and Sylvanus G. Morley, from the translation of Adrián Recinos. Norman: University of Oklahoma Press, 1991.

Proskouriakoff, Tatiana. *An Album of Maya Architecture*. Norman: University of Oklahoma Press, 1963.

Ramos, Carolyn. *The Art of Mexico*. Dubuque, Iowa: Kendall/Hunt Publishing, 1988.

Reents-Budet, Dorie. "Maya Civilization prior to European Contact." In *The Modern Maya*, by Macduff Everton. Albuquerque: University of New Mexico Press, 1991.

Ruz, Alberto. "An Astonishing Discovery: The Noble's Tomb at Palenque." In *The World of the Past*, edited by Jacquetta Hawkes. New York: Alfred A. Knopf, 1963.

Sabloff, Jeremy A.:
The Cities of Ancient Mexico. New York: Thames and Hudson, 1989.
The New Archaeology and the Ancient Maya. New York: Scientific American Library, 1990.

Scheffler, Lillian. *Uxmal, Kabáh, Sayil, Labná*. Guidebook. Mexico City: Panorama Editorial, S.A., 1988.

Schele, Linda, and David Freidel. *A Forest of Kings*. New York: William Morrow, 1990.

Schele, Linda, and Mary Ellen Miller. *The Blood of Kings*. Fort Worth, Tex.: Kimbell Art Museum, 1986.

Sharer, Robert J. "The Preclassic Origin of Lowland Maya States." Chapter 9 in *New Theories on the Ancient Maya*, edited by Elin C. Danien and Robert J. Sharer. Philadelphia: University Museum, University of Pennsylvania, 1992.

Sodi Morales, Demetrio. *The Maya World*. Mexico City: Minutiae Mexicana, 1991.

Spinden, Herbert J. *A Study of Maya Art*. New York: Dover Publications, 1975.

Stephens, John L.:
Incidents of Travel in Central America, Chiapas, and Yucatan (2 vols.). New York: Dover Publications, 1969.
Incidents of Travel in Yucatan (2 vols.). New York: Dover Publications, 1963.

Stierlin, Henri. *Art of the Maya*. New York: Rizzoli, 1981.

Stuart, Gene S. *America's Ancient Cities*. Washington, D.C.: National Geographic Society, 1988.

Stuart, George E. "Quest for Decipherment: A Historical and Biographical Survey of Maya Hieroglyphic Investigation." Chapter 1 in *New Theories on the Ancient Maya*, edited by Elin C. Danien and Robert J. Sharer. Philadelphia: University Museum, University of Pennsylvania, 1992.

Stuart, George E., and Gene S. Stuart:
Discovering Man's Past in the Americas. Washington, D.C.: National Geographic Society, 1973.
The Mysterious Maya. Washington, D.C.: National Geographic Society, 1977.

Suárez, Luis. *The Yucatan of the Mayas*. Translated by R. Kelly and Pilar P. Valdelomar. León, Spain: Editorial Everest, S.A., 1980.

Thompson, J. Eric S.:
"The Fall of Classic Mayan Civilization." In *The World of the Past*, edited by Jacquetta Hawkes. New York: Alfred A. Knopf, 1963.
Maya History and Religion. Norman: University of Oklahoma Press, 1990.

Trout, Lawana Hooper. *The Maya*. New York: Chelsea House Publishers, 1991.

Varela G., Elizabeth. *Uxmal*. Mexico City: Ediciones Alducin, 1985.

Von Hagen, Victor Wolfgang. *Frederick Catherwood, Architect*. New York: Oxford University Press, 1950.

Willard, T. A. *The City of the Sacred Well*. New York: Century Company, 1926.

PERIODICALS

Andrews, Anthony P. "The Maya Rediscovered." *Natural History*, October 1991.

Aveni, Anthony F., Sharon L. Gibbs, and Horst Hartung. "The Caracol Tower at Chichén Itzá: An Ancient Astronomical Observatory?" *Science*, June 1975.

Brady, James E., and George Veni. "Man-Made and Pseudo-Karst Caves: The Implications of Subsurface Features within Maya Centers." *Geoarchaeology: An International Journal*, 1992, Vol. 7.

Carlson, John B. "America's Ancient Skywatchers." *National Geographic*, March 1990.

Coe, Michael D. "A Triumph of Spirit." *Archaeology*, September/October 1991.

Coe, William R. "Resurrecting the Grandeur of Tikal." *National Geographic*, December 1975.

Dávalos, Eusebio Hurtado. "Into the Well of Sacrifice: Return to the Sacred Cenote." *National Geographic*, October 1961.

Fash, Barbara W. "Late Classic Architectural Sculpture Themes in Copan." *Ancient Mesoamerica*, Spring 1992.

Fash, William L. Jr., and Barbara W. Fash. "Scribes, Warriors, and Kings: The Lives of the Copán Maya." *Archaeology*, May/June 1990.

Fash, William L., et al. "The Hieroglyphic Stairway and Its Ancestors: Investigations of Copan Structure 10L-26." *Ancient Mesoamerica*, Spring 1992.

Fasquelle, Ricardo Agurcia, and William L. Fash, Jr.:
"Copán: A Royal Tomb Discovered." *National Geographic*, October 1989.
"Maya Artistry Unearthed." *National Geographic*, September 1991.

Hammond, Norman:
"Precious Stone of Grace." *Natural History*, August 1991.
"Unearthing the Oldest Known Maya." *National Geographic*, July 1982.

Hansen, Richard D. "The Maya Rediscov-

ered." *Natural History,* May 1991.
Jones, Christopher. "Maya Hieroglyphs." *Expedition,* 1985, Vol. 27.
LaFay, Howard. "The Maya, Children of Time." *National Geographic,* December 1975.
Littlehales, Bates. "Into the Well of Sacrifice: Return to the Sacred Cenote." *National Geographic,* October 1961.
McConahay, Mary Jo. "Arthur Demarest and the Temple of Doom." *Image (San Francisco Examiner* Sunday magazine), August 4, 1991.
Reents-Budet, Dorie. "The Discovery of a Ceramic Artist and Royal Patron among the Classic Maya." *Mexicon,* November 1987.
Rice, Don S. "The Maya Rediscovered." *Natural History,* February 1991.
Roberts, David. "The Decipherment of Ancient Maya." *The Atlantic Monthly,* September 1991.
Ruz, Alberto Lhuillier. "The Mystery of the Temple of the Inscriptions." Translated by J. Alden Mason. *Archaeology,* Spring 1953.
Sabloff, Jeremy A. "The Maya Rediscovered." *Natural History,* January 1991.
Schele, Linda. "The Maya Rediscovered." *Natural History,* November 1991.

Stuart, George E.:
"City of Kings and Commoners." *National Geographic,* October 1989.
"Riddle of the Glyphs." *National Geographic,* December 1975.
Ward, Fred. "Jade: Stone of Heaven." *National Geographic,* September 1987.

OTHER SOURCES
"Archaeological Prints." Catalog. Kensington, Calif.: John Wolf Prints, 1992.
Banta, Melissa, and Curtis M. Hinsley. "From Site to Sight." Catalog. Cambridge, Mass.: Peabody Museum, 1986.
Brady, James E. "The Petexbatun Regional Cave Survey: Ritual and Sacred Geography." Paper presented at 47th International Congress of Americanists, New Orleans, July 7-11, 1991.
Couch, N. C. Christopher. "Precolumbian Arts from the Ernest Erickson Collection." Catalog. New York: American Museum of Natural History, 1988.
Deletaille, Emile. "Trésors du Nouveau Monde." Catalog. Brussels: Musées Royaux d'Art et d'Histoire, 1992.
Demarest, Arthur A. "Warfare, Demography, and Tropical Ecology: Speculations on the Parameters of the Maya Collapse." Paper presented at the 89th

annual meeting of the American Anthropological Association, November 1990.
"Die Welt der Maya." Catalog. Mainz: Verlag Philipp von Zabern, 1992.
Giles, Sue, and Jennifer Steward (Eds.). "The Art of Ruins." Catalog. Bristol, England: City of Bristol Museum and Art Gallery, 1989.
Kowalski, Jeff Karl:
"Uxmal: The Regional Capital of the Eastern PUUC District." Paper prepared for the session Capital Centers in Pre-Columbian America, Annual Meeting of the College Art Association, Northern Illinois University, 1991.
"The PUUC as Seen from Uxmal." Paper prepared for the First Maler Symposium on Archaeology of Northwest Yucatan, Bonn, Germany, August 1990.
Parsons, Lee A., John B. Carlson, and Peter David Joralemon. "The Face of Ancient America." Catalog. Indianapolis: Indianapolis Museum of Art, 1988.
Rensberger, Boyce. "Maya Sculpture Is Largest Found." *Washington Post,* March 9, 1992.
Wilford, John Noble. "What Doomed the Maya? Maybe Warfare Run Amok." *New York Times,* November 19, 1991.

INDEX

on Maya, 25-28; photographic display by, *24*
Long Count calendar: 127-128, 137
Lord Chac: 142, 143
Loten, Stanley: sketched reconstructions of Tikal by, *74-77*
Lothrop, Samuel K.: 135
Lounsbury, Floyd: 90

M

MacArthur Foundation: 100
Madrid Codex: 32; pages from, *28-29*
Maia: 14
Main Acropolis (Copán): 93
Maler, Teobert: photographic reconstruction by, 40; photographs of Maya ruins by, *40-41;* at Tikal, 76
Mani: 148
Matheny, Ray: 60
Mathews, Peter: 70
Maudslay, Alfred P.: 18, 101; on difficulties of excavations in jungles of Central America, 22; photographs of Maya ruins by, *35, 36-37, 38, 39, 44-45, 94*
Maximilian, Emperor: 40
Maya: agricultural methods, 12, 58-60; architectural features of, 12, *17,* 20, 25, 51, 55, 56, 71, 76, 126, 127, 128, 131, 133, 135, 136, 137, *140-141,* 142; astronomical observations by, 12, *17,* 63, 129, *130-131, 132-133;* bows and arrows, first appearance of, 148; calendars, 12, 14, 15, *30,* 126, 127-128, 131, 160; caves, religious use of, 104-105, 139; censers, *71, 118;* ceremonial cities, 33, 58; chert weapons of, 47, 48; Classic period of, 50, 52 70, 73, 82, 90, 93, 105, 108, 127, 137; codices, 13, *28-29,* 32, *131, 133;* court life of, *108-109;* culture suppressed by Spanish, 16-17; decline of, 12, 90, 92, 102, 104-106, 127, 161; differences between northern and southern Maya, 126-127; dogs, symbolic role of, 159; domain of, *map end paper,* 9-12, 126-127, 160-161; Early Classic period, 160; ecological problems of, 96, 103, 104, 106; emergence of sophisticated economy, 148; European diseases, impact of, 15; food staples and diet, 28, 51, 155; funeral rites, 89; gold ornaments, *124;* head binding, 20, 54-55; and human sacrifice, 47-49, 51, 65, 70, 71, 72, 79, 85-86, *92,* 96, 114, 116, *117,* 119-120, 123-124, 129, 139-142; irrigation systems of, 60, 144-145; kingship, 65-68, 69, 70, 82, 90, 93, 99, 102, 136, 141, 142, 160; Late Classic period, 140, 161; literature, 16, 56-57; malnutrition and disease, growing incidence of, 103; mathematics, 12, *17;* modern-day descendants of, *149;* music and dance, *110-111;* myths of, 29, 84, 91, 114, 149; numbers, *30,* 33, 52, 79; number seals, 49; ocarina, *53;* oligarchic rule, 127, 136; origins of, 12, 50, 53,

160-161; peak population estimates for, 10; peasantry, 28, 76; political organization and religious ideology, 57, 95; Postclassic period, 161; Preclassic period, 160; rediscovery of by adventurers and early archaeologists, 7-9, 18-25; religious beliefs and ceremonies, 55, 56, 57, 61, 62-63, 79, 95, 104-105, 107, 110, 113, 148, 149, 159; renewal of urban centers, 61-62; ritual ball game and courts, 12, *95, 114-115,* 129, 142; ritual bloodletting, 48, 53, 62-63, *66, 67,* 69, 71, 91, 101, *113;* road networks of, 127, 137, 138, 144; scribes, esteem for, 97; societal rise in sophistication, 13; Spanish conquest, 14-16, 150, 161; Spanish initial contacts with, 14-15; speculative theories on origins of, 21, 25, 121; stratified class system of, 12, 49, 54, 107, 108, 160; temples, cross section of, *17, 78-79;* terra-cotta stamp, *52;* throne mat *(pop),* 70; time, concerns for, 33; tombs of, 82, 88-89, *96-97,* 105-106, 126, 160; trade by, 10, 54, 61, *map* 64, 71, 106, 124, 127, 135, 160; trade goods, *65;* trading centers of, 62, 68, 73, 138, 150; transformation of farming and trading villages into ceremonial centers, 48-49, 53; urban centers of, 9; use of intoxicating brews and plants, 112, 113; warfare by, 65, 68, 70-72, 93, 106, *116-117,* 127, 128, 135, 136, 143, 150, 161; weaving, *149;* women and social structure, 69, 107
Maya Indians: 9
Mayapán: 126, 136; Chichén Itzá sacked by, 127, 145; decline of, 148-150; estimated peak population of, 148; inferiority of construction at, 145-146; rise of, 137, 161
Mérida: 121; hieroglyphic books found near, 16
Moon-Zero-Bird: 70
Morley, Sylvanus G.: 48; excavations at Chichén Itzá, 134, *135;* on Maya inscriptions, 33
Motagua River: 52

N

Nakbé: 61, 160; excavations at, 54-56; massive construction at, 57-58; pyramids at, 54, 55-56, 58, 62
Naranjo: pottery from, *68, 69*
National Geographic Society: 137
National Institute of Anthropology and History (Mexico): 83, 137
New River: 60, 65
Nickerson, Ephraim: 122
North Acropolis (Tikal): *74, 75*
Northern Illinois University: 143
Nunnery (Uxmal): 142; Chac mask at, *140*

O

Obsidian: Maya regard for, 101; trade in, 61; use in tools, 60

Olmecs: and jade, 52; and the Maya, 53, 160
Owens, John: *45*

P

Pacal: 90, 91, 92, 161; jade mask, *87;* sarcophagus cover, *84;* skeleton of, *86;* stucco head from tomb of, *85;* tomb of, 82, *83, 87-89*
Pacheco, Arturo Romano: 86
Palace of Labná: *144-145, 146-147*
Palace of Sayil: *147*
Palace of the Governor (Uxmal): *10,* 139, *140-141,* 142
Palace of the Masks (Kabah): 143
Palenque: 34, 100, 105, 126, 139, 161; carved panel (Temple of the Sun), *18-19;* construction at under Pacal and Can-Balam, 90; decline of, 92, 104; early visitors to, 20-21; excavation of Pacal's tomb, 81-89; grave goods found at, 85, *86, 87;* pyramids and palace at, *8-9, 17, 18, 36-37, 40-41, 82;* rediscovery of by del Rio, 18-19; Stephens and Catherwood at, 23-25; temple at, 18, *40-41, 82;* tower at, *36-37, 82;* women rulers of, 107
Paris Codex: 29
Peabody Museum: 28, 33, 35, 40, 45, 121, 125
Pennsylvania State University: 104
Petén rain forest: 73; stucco mask discovered in, *6*
Petexbatun: exploration of Maya caves in, 104
Piedras Negras: reconstruction of acropolis at, *88-89;* steles at, 34, *40*
Pollock, H. E. D.: excavations at Mayapán, 147-148
Pop (throne mat): 70
Popol Vuh: 29, 32, *56-57, 114*
Pottery: bowl found at Cuello, *52;* carved ceramics, *112-113;* ceramic head, *46;* grave goods, *68, 69, 97,* 105; at Nakbé, 54; painted ceramic figurines, *cover;* painted vases, 71; photo rollout images from, *108, 116;* polychrome bowl, *160;* polychrome pots produced at Naranjo, *68, 69;* production methods used for, 151; tripod vessel, *154*
Princeton University: 100
Principal Bird Deity: *See* Celestial Bird
Proskouriakoff, Tatiana: *33,* 88; Chichén Itzá, illustrations by, *88-89, 120,* 121; studies on Maya hieroglyphs, 34
Psychic duct: 89
Putun Maya: 134
Puuc Hills: *end paper,* 143, 161; Maya cities in, 126-127, 139, *140-141,* 142-145

Q

Quetzalcoatl: 127
Quetzals: decorative use of, 53
Quiché Maya: 29
Quiriguá: 36, 99, 100; stele at, *38, 39*

N

• Tula

• Teotihuacan

• La Venta

GULF OF MEXICO

CARIBBEAN SEA

PACIFIC OCEAN

PACIFIC OCEAN

Mexico

Beltze

Guatemala

Honduras

El Salvador

0   100 miles